The Mysteries of Beethoven's HAIR

The Mysteries of

Beethoven's HAIR

Russell Martin *and* Lydia Nibley

Charlesbridge

For Alex Nibley

Text copyright © 2009 by Russell Martin and Lydia Nibley
Illustrations copyright © by individual copyright holders

Published by Charlesbridge
85 Main Street
Watertown, MA 02472
(617) 926-0329
www.charlesbridge.com

Library of Congress Cataloging-in-Publication Data
Martin, Russell, 1952–
    The mysteries of Beethoven's hair / Russell Martin and Lydia Nibley
        p. cm.
    ISBN 978-1-57091-714-1 (reinforced for library use)
1. Beethoven, Ludwig van, 1770–1827—Relics—Juvenile literature.
2. Beethoven, Ludwig van, 1770–1827—Biography—Juvenile literature.
I. Nibley, Lydia. II. Title.
ML3930.B4M37 2009
780.92—dc22   2008007257

Printed in the United States of America
(hc) 10 9 8 7 6 5 4 3 2 1

Display type and text type set in Centaur MT and Adobe Caslon
Color separations by Chroma Graphics, Singapore
Printed and bound by Lake Book Manufacturing, Inc.
Production supervision by Brian G. Walker
Designed by Diane M. Earley

Contents

Oh, it would be so lovely to live a thousand lives.

Ludwig van Beethoven

Utterly deaf and isolated from interaction with others, Beethoven often walked alone through the streets of Vienna, composing music in his head.

One

Beethoven: A Lock of Hair

*L*udwig van Beethoven's hair spread wildly out from his head and blew in all directions as he took his daily stroll through the city of Vienna. He had a habit of clasping his hands behind his back, his head thrusting forward, and he walked in an odd, lumbering way. His expression was often foreboding, and his eyes appeared small but bright. His complexion was dark and his face had been pockmarked by smallpox when he was a boy. Although his mind was full of music, he could not hear the noise of the great city in which he trod. The deafness that years before had begun to rob him of subtle sounds by now had reduced his world to silence, and he could hear only the music he imagined.

Yet Ludwig van Beethoven, this strange figure who sometimes was mistaken for a tramp because his clothes were dirty and his appearance so disheveled, was actually the most celebrated composer in the world.

1

The grand city of Vienna was the musical capital of the world and Beethoven's adopted home, a place where he achieved his greatest triumphs and suffered his deepest defeats.

In a time without film or television or recorded music, live performances provided the only opportunity for people to hear and appreciate music. What we now call "classical" music was an art form that was enormously important in the lives of the privileged and unfortunate alike, and composers like Beethoven often were seen as little less than gods. Newspapers wrote obsessively about musicians and composers, and huge crowds gathered outside concert halls when a new work was being performed. Despite his deafness and his strange ways, Beethoven had premiered his Ninth Symphony to huge approval, and people believed his bold, passionate, and revolutionary music would endure for centuries.

As Beethoven walked in Vienna, he couldn't possibly have imagined that on his death, a lock of his hair would take an amazing trip through time, and that it would answer the question of why he suffered so many illnesses.

Like the bones of ancient Christian martyrs that were considered sacred, and like the venerated bodies of deceased Tibetan Buddhist Dalai Lamas, a particular lock of Beethoven's hair would become a very important relic, a physical remnant of a once-living human being that kept the spirit of that person present and powerfully alive for others.

How fitting that the wild mane that had framed his face and made him instantly recognizable would unlock some of the secrets of his body, mind, and unruly temperament, and perhaps even explain something about his genius. This lock of hair would survive to tell a true and extraordinary story.

Dr. Alfredo "Che" Guevara and Ira Brilliant

Two

The Detective Work Begins

*O*n a bright December morning in 1995, a bit of Beethoven's hair that had come from Europe to Arizona was causing quite a stir. The two men to whom the lock of the great composer's hair now belonged—Ira Brilliant, a retired real estate developer, and a Mexican American physician named Alfredo "Che" Guevara—had been joined by many others, including television crews from local stations and from as far away as London. They had all gathered to watch the opening of the dark wood oval frame in which a lock of Beethoven's hair was sealed behind glass. The wood locket was about four inches long, and the coil of brown and gray hair inside it was capturing everyone's attention.

On old paper that had been glued to the flat back of the locket, someone named Paul Hiller long ago had written the

This inscription by Paul Hiller was discovered on the back of the locket that held Beethoven's hair. It provided the date when Paul's father cut the hair and described when the locket was passed down to him.

following words in German: "This hair was cut off Beethoven's corpse by my father, Dr. Ferdinand v. Hiller, on the day after Ludwig van Beethoven's death, that is, on 27 March 1827, and was given to me as a birthday present in Cologne on 1 May 1883."

While Ira Brilliant and the others watched with fascination, Dr. Guevara, dressed in green surgical scrubs and wearing a mask and gloves, worked at a sterile table, a sharp scalpel in his hand. In a way this was a surgery, and the doctor proceeded carefully. "Now I'm slicing through the last of the glue that holds the paper backing," he announced.

A video camera looked down from overhead. The rest of the group watched the doctor's work on television monitors placed around the room. Everyone was surprised when the first layer of paper came away and more writing was found on another piece of very old and brittle paper underneath. Handwritten in German, these words had been written by a picture framer who had refurbished the locket. And now, many years later, a doctor was carefully cutting this final layer of paper. It came away in one piece, and then he gently pried the locket open with a scalpel. "Wow, could you hear that?" Dr. Guevara asked. "I heard a rush of air like a vacuum when I started to separate the glass." And when the two pieces of glass were pulled apart, there it was—Beethoven's hair—exposed to the world.

As they talked to reporters, Brilliant and Guevara outlined the scientific tests they planned to have conducted on the hair— tests they hoped would determine what drugs and minerals had been in Beethoven's system at the time of his death. High levels of zinc might mean that his immune system had been severely damaged and that his body was trying to compensate. If they found high levels of mercury, this could indicate that he had been treated for a significant infection, since mercury was the common remedy prescribed by doctors at the time. If they found toxic levels of mercury in Beethoven's system, this might help explain his very eccentric behavior. Lots of lead in his hair could point to a potential cause of the composer's deafness and of the terrible stomach pain he had endured throughout his life.

The chemical profile of Beethoven's body at the time of his death would provide important information to scientists and musicologists, yet the newspaper and television reporters wanted to know more than what tests would be run and why. They wanted to know what it was about Beethoven that so obsessed these two men.

"My interest in Beethoven is like a fire burning inside me," answered the grandfatherly and energetic seventy-three-year-old Ira Brilliant, who had been buying letters written by Beethoven and first editions of Beethoven's music for years. He had accumulated a significant collection of material before he and Dr. Guevara set out to purchase Beethoven's hair.

A large man with thick black hair atop his head, his speech filled with echoes of his native Spanish, Dr. Guevara was obviously obsessed with both Beethoven's music and Beethoven the man. "Beethoven was deaf, as you know. He suffered from kidney stones, which is a very painful condition. He had hepatitis; he had multiple episodes of gastrointestinal infections. For someone to have that many maladies and to suffer so greatly and yet produce superhuman music, music that can actually elevate the spirit to a much different plane than the ordinary plane we live in, is quite phenomenal. To get this close to a man who was able to do this . . . for me it's a personal triumph. Acquiring the hair already has changed my life."

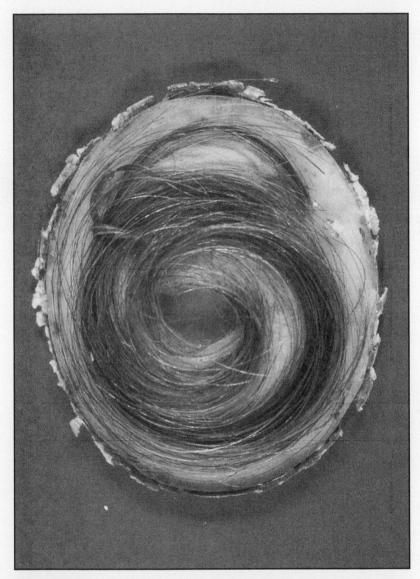

The lock of Beethoven's hair remained in a coil after Dr. Guevara removed it from the locket in which it was placed in 1827.

Beethoven as a young man on his first trip to Vienna.

Three

Beethoven:
A Young & Extraordinary Talent

*L*udwig van Beethoven was named for his grandfather, the music director of the court of Maximilian Friedrich. Although Beethoven was not quite three when his grandfather died, in later years he imagined that his huge talents must have been passed down from his brilliant grandfather. Beethoven's father, Johann, was a tenor in the court choir; he taught singing and was a passably good pianist and violinist as well, but his career in music did not seem very bright, and he was not promoted to a higher position.

Beethoven's mother, Maria van Beethoven, was intelligent, patient, and kind, in contrast to her husband, who had a terrible temper and was an alcoholic. Beethoven's father often bullied his son, beating him on occasion, and dragging the crying and frightened boy from his bed to make him practice the piano late into the night. It is easy to imagine that his father's rages might have affected the boy's love of music—that the young Beethoven could have turned away from his talent in rebellion against his father—but instead, Beethoven endured the harsh treatment and developed his remarkable talents.

⤜⬥⬥⤛

Beethoven was a natural musician and had barely reached the age of seven when he gave his first performance on the piano. At eight he began to receive piano, violin, and viola instruction from a series of noted court musicians, and when he was only eleven he became the deputy to the court organist Christian Gottlob Neefe.

In this role, Beethoven played the organ at church services and court functions when Neefe was absent, and in turn Neefe nurtured and encouraged his talented young student in every way he could. Neefe, a compassionate, cultivated, and well-read man, was more like Beethoven's grandfather than his father. He took young Beethoven under his wing and arranged for the boy to study music in Vienna, Europe's musical capital, where Neefe hoped Beethoven would mature into an extraordinary musician. Perhaps Neefe also hoped to keep Beethoven safely away from his abusive father as well.

In Vienna Beethoven studied intently and, on one April afternoon, the young teenage boy from Bonn was asked to play

On his first visit to Vienna, Beethoven played for Mozart, who remarked, "Keep your eyes on that one; someday he will give the world plenty to talk about."

for the great Mozart. Beethoven performed a complicated piece, but Mozart was somewhat unimpressed—surely there were dozens of people who could master one showy composition. Beethoven wanted to demonstrate what he was capable of, and so he asked Mozart to give him a musical theme on which he might improvise. Mozart provided a brief theme and Beethoven expanded it brilliantly, showing an astounding range in his spontaneous composition and exhibiting inventiveness and incredible power. Mozart was astonished and, as he left the room to speak with the courtiers he had kept waiting, he said, "Keep your eyes on that one; someday he will give the world plenty to talk about."

Beethoven would probably have met Mozart again, or even perhaps had the opportunity to study with him, but his time in Vienna was abruptly cut short by news from Bonn that his mother was gravely ill with tuberculosis. After traveling for several days, he was able to reach her bedside and spend time with her before she died. Her death was a terrible blow to the whole family. Beethoven's infant sister, Maria Margaretha, died a few months later, and the family would never be the same. Two younger brothers were now left in Ludwig's care, and his father simply drank himself into a total collapse.

When his father lost his job with the court, Beethoven, who was only eighteen at the time, successfully petitioned the court to grant him half of his father's former salary in order to support his two brothers, his father, and himself. He was the head of the household now, and would have to make the most of the musical education he had received in order to feed and clothe his family and keep a roof over their heads.

Beethoven played viola in the orchestras of the court chapel and theater and became friends with other young musicians.

He also had the good fortune to meet a prominent and progressive family headed by the dynamic young widow Hélène von Breuning. The Breuning family was spirited and intellectually curious, and Beethoven was made to feel as if he was part of this lively and interesting family. He was introduced to the thrilling new notions of reform, freedom, and brotherhood known as the Enlightenment, and these ideas influenced Beethoven's music throughout his life. He was already being called a musical genius, and by now he had been commissioned to compose the music for a folk ballet and two cantatas, one commemorating the death of the much-loved Emperor Joseph II, and one in celebration of his successor, Leopold II.

Beethoven worked very hard, and when he was exhausted and ill, which happened often, Frau von Breuning took care of him. She treated him like her own son, and when he was seized with bad tempers and brooding silences, she did her best to encourage him and to buoy up his self-confidence, understanding that Beethoven could, at times, be almost paralyzed with shyness, moodiness, and self-doubt.

The mentors and friends who supported Beethoven's musical and intellectual development wanted to make sure that he was stimulated and that he would have the additional training and support needed to achieve his potential. His supporters realized that in order for Beethoven's talent to be more widely recognized, he must return to the heart of the musical world—to the great city of Vienna. The revolution in France that had begun three years before had now led to rumors of war across much of Europe. The new French regime had declared war on Austria, and Beethoven had to leave Bonn quickly in order to travel safely to Vienna. As he left, he carried with him an album filled with written good wishes from his family, friends, and the patrons who hoped he would fulfill his great musical promise.

Four

The Better Medicine

*T*he opening of the locket in Tucson, Arizona, on that December day in 1995 had quickly led to new revelations. As the group had expected, the hair inside it appeared approximately two hundred years old, forensic anthropologist Walter Birkby declared. And under microscopic examination, Birkby also noted the presence of a few follicles at the roots of individual hairs, meaning that DNA testing would likely be possible.

Then Birkby startled Ira Brilliant and Dr. Che Guevara by revealing that the lock's presumed 150–200 hairs actually numbered 582. They were pleased that the boy who had snipped this lock of hair from Beethoven's corpse had taken so many strands. Brilliant and Dr. Guevara decided that the Beethoven Center at San José State University in California

17

would receive 422 individual hairs. Most of the lock of hair would now be on display with the rest of the Beethoven collection, in a place where Beethoven scholars and adults and children from all over the world could study the composer and his music.

Dr. Guevara claimed 160 strands for himself, some of which would be needed for the forensic testing. Dr. Guevara simply put the hairs that now belonged to him inside a sterile Petri dish, its lid held fast with a silver ribbon. He placed the glass dish inside his fireproof office safe. A bit of Beethoven's hair would be nearby as he saw his patients each day.

Guevara shipped twenty hairs to Dr. Werner Baumgartner, head of Psychemedics Corporation in Los Angeles, who completed a drug analysis of the hairs. Baumgartner and his colleagues at Psychemedics had tested more than two million human hair samples over the years using a procedure capable of detecting the presence of even small amounts of morphine, heroin, and other opiates. And they had proven scientifically that trace amounts of opiates remained stable in human hair over very long periods of time.

If Beethoven had taken opiates to numb his pain in the last months of his life, evidence of that fact certainly would be revealed by the chemistry of his hair. But what Baumgartner found instead—or what he didn't find—was very surprising. To analyze the hair, Baumgartner carefully washed it, examining it to make sure that any potential contamination had been removed from the outside of the hair. Then Baumgartner liquefied the hair—a process that released any molecules of drugs that were entrapped in the hair shaft itself after Beethoven had ingested them. The results of the analysis showed no opiates in any of the Beethoven hair he studied.

It was well-documented that Beethoven had seen the best doctors in the city during his final days, and it was logical to assume that he would have been offered morphine to ease his suffering, yet now it appeared that he had refused the drug. Confined to his bed and in terrible pain, he had continued to sketch musical ideas on pages strewn around him. Even on his deathbed, perhaps keeping his mind clear so that he could compose, music seemed to him to be the better medicine.

Beethoven tutored many piano students, most of them young women.
He longed for a deep romantic relationship, but his increasing deafness and
his complex personality prevented it.

Five

Beethoven: This Wretched Life

Although people were fascinated by his emotional and passionate music, many found it hard to truly *like* Ludwig van Beethoven. He was often rude, his moods vacillated wildly, and he was a difficult person to be around. Those who knew him well understood that it was almost impossible to meet his demands or to make him happy.

Beethoven boasted in a letter sent to a friend in 1792, soon after he moved to Vienna, "Not only as an artist but also as a man you will find me better and more developed." But when the friend visited Beethoven in Vienna, he found a man who was self-obsessed and tactless, and who could also be very petty. Beethoven exhibited a boyish sense of humor and could be very kind on occasion, but he tended to wear out his friends and colleagues with his emotional outbursts and bad temper.

Beethoven repeatedly fell in love with women who were already married, or who were of a much higher social position, which, in that time and place, made a relationship nearly impossible. In order for him to marry above his station, a woman would have had to love him enough to weather the storm of her family's disapproval. No woman Beethoven set his sights on would have him as a husband, and this was difficult for him to bear. For Beethoven, even simple friendships with women were complicated, because he was likely to call a friend a "false dog" one day and then, within a day or two, address her as "Dear Little Ignaz of my Heart." Beethoven's expression of a wild range of emotion certainly enriched his musical gifts, but his personal life was troubled as a result of this instability.

The music Beethoven created was absolutely new, and was both confusing and thrilling to audiences and critics. He had separated his style from composers such as Haydn and Mozart and was experimenting with music that was groundbreaking and complex. Beethoven's piano sonatas were acknowledged as the work of a genius.

His Third Symphony was inspired by the tumultuous times in which he lived. This long and daring new work was to be titled *Bonaparte*, to honor what Napoleon Bonaparte had described as an effort to shape a liberated and new kind of Europe. But when Beethoven heard the news that the general Napoleon had declared himself emperor of France, he flew into a rage and tore the title page from the musical score. "Now he will trample on all human rights and indulge

Throughout his life Beethoven found both solace and inspiration in nature.

Beethoven's music was very popular with Vienna's wealthy elite, yet it was also quite revolutionary.

only his own ambition. He will place himself above everyone and become a tyrant," Beethoven said. He retitled the symphony *Eroica*.

Beethoven wanted to bring the world a kind of music that explored heroism and triumph over pain. He created music that reflected the hope of liberation and that addressed the reality of death, and in return for completing this difficult and challenging work, he experienced success. His opera *Fidelio* achieved great acclaim, and he was earning enough money to afford good wine, servants to care for his household, and attractive lodgings in Vienna, with trips to the country in the summer. People recognized him on the streets now, and his music brought him attention and respect, but Beethoven said to a friend, "It is a peculiar feeling to see and hear oneself praised and at the same time to realize one's own inferiority as fully as I do." During the time his career was expanding and he was reaching his potential as a composer, he was also privately suffering a wide range of illnesses and facing the devastating consequences of losing his hearing.

Much of Beethoven's fiery temper was explained by his consistently poor health. While still a teenager he had begun to be troubled by abdominal disease, and over the succeeding years he also had suffered intense headaches. He fought a series of abscesses and infections, pneumonia, and bronchitis, which in an age prior to the development of antibiotics were very serious and life-threatening illnesses.

When he returned to Vienna in 1792, he was plagued regularly with the abdominal pain, cramping, constipation, and diarrhea that then was labeled *kolik*. He suffered a prolonged and difficult bout of this illness in the year 1795; then in 1797 what was described as a "terrible typhus" befell him, causing a high fever that lasted for weeks. In the midst of these long illnesses, he was also losing his hearing. When at last he confessed his alarming deafness in an 1801 letter to his childhood friend Franz Wegeler, who now was a practicing physician in Bonn, Beethoven's health seemed to be collapsing.

For the last three years my hearing has become weaker and weaker. In the theater I have to place myself quite close to the orchestra in order to understand what the actor is saying, and at that distance I cannot hear the high notes of instruments or voices. As for the spoken word, it is surprising that some people have never noticed my deafness. But since I have always been liable to fits of absentmindedness, they attribute my hardness of hearing to that. Sometimes too I can scarcely hear a person who speaks softly. I can hear sounds, it is true, but I cannot make out the words. Heaven alone knows what is to become of me.

Nine months later, in the village of Heiligenstadt on the banks of the Danube River not far from Vienna—where he had gone in hopes that being away from the noise of the city might allow his ears to recover—Beethoven had grown deeply depressed. He was overwhelmed with grief about his growing deafness and felt hopeless about his future. Resting had done nothing to help his dreadful hearing, and on October 6, 1802, he addressed to his two brothers a long, emotional letter that was a plea for understanding.

For six years now I have had an incurable condition . . . and yet it was impossible for me to say to people, "Speak louder, shout, for I am deaf." Ah, how could I possibly admit weakness of the one sense which should be more perfect in me than others?

In this Heiligenstadt apartment, Beethoven wrote an impassioned letter to his brothers, in which he expressed the hope that someone would be able to explain his deafness one day.

Beethoven explained in the letter that it was humiliating when someone standing near him heard a flute or a shepherd singing in the distance and he could hear nothing. Not being able to hear brought him to the point of despair.

Many experts suggest that Beethoven's illnesses and deafness, together with his enormous talent and appreciation of nature, play a central role in the profundity of his music.

A little more and I would have ended my life. Only my art held me back. Ah, it seemed to me impossible to leave the world until I had produced all that I felt was within me; and so I spared this wretched life. . . . As soon as I am dead, if Dr. Schmidt is still alive, ask him in my name to describe my disease, and attach this written document to his account of my illness, so that at least as much as possible the world may be reconciled to me.

Still two months away from his thirty-second birthday, Ludwig van Beethoven had come to believe that his life—or at least the life that mattered to him—was almost too painful to be endured. He had accomplished much in the decade he had lived in Vienna, including establishing a reputation as the finest pianist his adopted city ever had seen, and he was known as a composer of the very first rank. By now he had composed more than two dozen piano sonatas, violin sonatas, piano trios, string quartets, a piano quintet, a piano concerto, a C major symphony, as well as a new symphony in D major, on which he currently was at work.

Yet none of his musical triumphs seemed to matter. His hearing was being robbed from him, and he made it clear that he would have responded by killing himself, were it not for the music that he believed he was still destined to compose.

With this realization, he had little choice but to return to his life in the noisy city whose sounds increasingly were lost to him, and he resolved to draw the music out of himself, even though he knew it would be very difficult. In the letter written to his brothers, he attempted to share the terrible truth about his life, his sense of hopelessness, and his renewed determination to create music, but then, rather than sending the letter to them—and for reasons that were never explained—Beethoven folded the paper and tucked it away in his desk, showing it to no one for the rest of his life.

Who could have imagined that, not long after Beethoven's death, the letter would be discovered, and that nearly 170 years later two men in Arizona would set out to fulfill Beethoven's heartfelt request? Brilliant and Guevara would ask scientists to test a lock of Beethoven's hair in hopes that, at last, the world would have an explanation for the composer's deafness, his emotional difficulties, and his life of disease. This information would help the world understand Beethoven more completely, which was his own deep desire.

Six

The Boy Who Cut Beethoven's Hair

*T*he fifteen-year-old musical protégé Ferdinand Hiller made a snowy journey to see Beethoven in Vienna in March 1827 with his piano and composition instructor Johann Nepomuk Hummel. Hummel had heard the news that his friend, fifty-six-year-old Ludwig van Beethoven, was dying, and he wanted to see Beethoven again. He also hoped his gifted young student might be inspired by spending time in the company of the great composer before he was gone.

When they arrived they found Beethoven looking very pale and gaunt, his thick hair uncombed. He received them warmly and spoke of unfinished musical projects and hopes for the future, while also being fully aware of his present condition. He faintly whispered, "I shall, no doubt, soon be going above."

The boy and his teacher returned to see Beethoven three more times over the next two weeks before Beethoven finally surrendered his life of relentless pain. On the day of their final visit, Beethoven's condition had become very grave. "He lay, weak and miserable, sighing deeply at intervals," Hiller wrote. "Not a word fell from his lips; sweat stood out on his forehead. His handkerchief not being conveniently at hand, Hummel's wife took her fine cambric handkerchief and dried his face again and again. Never shall I forget the grateful glance with which his broken eyes looked upon her."

Three days later the boy and his teacher received the sad news that Beethoven had died in the midst of a dramatic afternoon storm. When they returned to Beethoven's home a day later to pay their final respects, Beethoven's face appeared very different, frozen in its mask of death, but at least it was obvious that the great man was finally at rest.

Beethoven's body still lay in his bedroom and had been placed in an oak coffin that stood on a brass stand, his head resting on a white silk pillow. His long hair had been combed and was crowned with a wreath of white roses. The two did not remain for long beside the coffin, but before they left, young Hiller asked his teacher if he could cut a lock of the master composer's hair. In the days before photography, people commonly took locks of hair as remembrances of the dead, and other locks of hair, it was obvious, had already been cut from Beethoven's head. Hummel quietly whispered yes to his student, and the two of them were moved by the deep sadness of the moment.

Ferdinand Hiller took the scissors he had brought with him, lifted a small lock of Beethoven's long, half-gray hair, pulled it away from his head, and cut it free.

This plaster death mask of Ludwig van Beethoven was made the day after his death. In the era before photography, death masks—as well as locks of hair— were valued as physical mementos of people.

The boy who cut the lock of hair, Ferdinand Hiller, had been born in Frankfurt in 1811, the son of a prominent merchant who had changed his last name from Hildesheim to Hiller in order to help conceal his Jewish identity at a time when persecution against Jews was rising dangerously in Europe. But Frankfurt itself was a relatively tolerant city, one in which Jews were able to live largely free from discrimination.

Ferdinand's parents were wealthy and very committed to the arts, and when the gifted boy was seven he began to take piano lessons from a famous pianist. Three years later, while only ten, Ferdinand performed in public for the first time, playing Mozart's Concerto in C Minor, and five years later he moved to Weimar to study with Hummel.

The boy's talents blossomed under Hummel's instruction, and he marveled at his good fortune. Because of Hummel the boy Hiller by now had even met the great Beethoven on his deathbed, and had attended the composer's somber funeral. As he watched his teacher throw three laurel wreaths onto the coffin that lay deep in the earth, Hiller remembered what Beethoven had told him a few days before. "Devote your life entirely to art," the dying man had encouraged him, and Hiller vowed that he would do so.

Ferdinand Hiller kept the lock of Beethoven's hair inside a small, oval wooden frame that had been painted black, the kind of locket in which miniature portraits often were displayed. The group of hairs had been looped into a loose coil and sealed between two pieces of glass. The treasured keepsake was now secure for those occasions when Hiller would show it to musical friends whom he was sure could appreciate how special it was to hold something of Beethoven himself in their hands.

———◦———

When Ferdinand Hiller turned seventeen in 1828, he moved alone to Paris to continue his musical training. Paris was a vital and stimulating place for a young artist to blossom. By the time Hiller settled there, so many young artists had moved to the City of Light that they had become collectively known as "Young France." Among them were writers such as Victor Hugo, Honoré de Balzac, the German poet Heinrich Heine, and the woman who dressed in men's clothing and went by the name George Sand; painters such as Eugène Delacroix; as well as an astonishing number of promising young musicians—the Polish-born pianist and composer Frédéric Chopin, German Felix Mendelssohn, Hungarian Franz Liszt, Italian Vincenzo Bellini, Frenchman Hector Berlioz—a great champion of Beethoven's music—and, of course, now Hiller himself.

This extraordinary group shared a deep belief in art that was emotionally expressive, and they believed that Beethoven and his music had carved a monumentally daring and pioneering path they hoped to follow far into the future.

The young, talented men and women enjoyed long hours together, attending concerts, eating and drinking, and sharing their compositions with each other. They loved to hear Hiller's stories about the times a few years before when he had actually met and spoken with the great Beethoven. Every time the locket of hair was reverently passed between them, each of the young artists was deeply moved to hold a literal bit of Beethoven in an open palm.

Ferdinand Hiller had become a composer and renowned musician in his own right when this portrait was taken. At age fifteen, Beethoven encouraged him to devote his life to art.

Eventually the pressure to build careers sent many in the group far from Paris, and Hiller too began a period in which he moved almost constantly, traveling—with the lock of hair always safely in his possession—throughout Italy and Germany before he accepted a position in 1850 as *Kapellmeister*, or director of music, in the city of Cologne, just a few miles from Beethoven's birthplace in Bonn. Ferdinand Hiller, his wife Antolka, an opera singer, and his cherished lock of Beethoven's hair had found a home.

For the next twenty years, Hiller was at the center of Cologne's rich musical life, and he accomplished many important goals. He created a music school, or conservatory, whose educational quality was respected throughout Germany. He established the city's renowned monthly concert series, as well as a summer music festival, bringing Europe's finest musicians and composers to Cologne. Yet for himself, Hiller said, "[M]y greatest joy, my greatest source of pride, was to be able to conduct so many marvelous performances of the Ninth Symphony of Beethoven."

But at those times when he was utterly honest with himself, Hiller also admitted to an enormous personal disappointment in the limits of his own musical talent. He had not become the towering composer he once believed he could be. Despite his significant abilities and his utter dedication, Hiller knew and understood that his music lacked something essential. It was his friend and fellow composer Robert Schumann who explained the problem all too succinctly: Hiller's music simply "lacked that triumphant power that we are unable to resist."

Beethoven's music, in contrast, had become increasingly admired during the more than forty years since his death, and Hiller himself explained why in a special issue of the magazine *Salon* that celebrated the hundredth anniversary of Beethoven's birth. The master's music remained unmatched, Hiller wrote, because it achieved "softness without weakness, enthusiasm without hollowness, longing without sentimentality, passion without madness." Hiller said Beethoven's music expressed great joy, but also noted that when it expressed the deepest suffering of humankind, the composer didn't lose himself in the suffering, but rather triumphed over it. Hiller wrote of Beethoven, ". . . never did an artist live whose creations were so truly new—his sphere was the unforeseen."

Seven

Passed from Father to Son

*F*erdinand Hiller grew heavy as he aged, and eventually his physical weight took a toll on his heart and circulatory system. As his health worsened, he put his affairs in order in preparation for the death that he sensed soon would come to him, offering his son, Paul—now an opera singer with a successful career—a great and important gift on the occasion of Paul's thirtieth birthday. Hiller wanted his only son to have and safeguard the locket in which so many years before he had placed the precious lock of Ludwig van Beethoven's hair. He suspected that dangerous times were coming to Europe, and he expressed deep concern about the future as he passed the treasured possession to his son.

Ferdinand Hiller was outraged when government-sanctioned violence against Jews in Russia led to increasingly hate-filled speech and anti-Jewish laws and attacks throughout Eastern Europe and in Germany as well. He grew deeply pessimistic about Europe's political future when he observed Jews being robbed of basic human rights. "I wonder whether you and I will really miss taking part in the next fifty years. I don't think so," he wrote to a friend. "A lot of blood will flow and men will not be human any more."

Hiller's health worsened, and then in 1885, seventy-three-year-old Ferdinand Hiller died, his head held in his son Paul's arms. He had succeeded wonderfully in his lifelong commitment to the importance of music. As Beethoven had encouraged him to do so many years before, he had devoted his life to art.

⇒•⇐

Ferdinand's son, Paul Hiller, continued to work as an opera singer and to safeguard the locket that contained Beethoven's hair, and in 1911, when he was in his fifties, he celebrated the hundredth anniversary of his late father's birth by making an unusual request of Cologne art dealer and frame maker Hermann Grosshennig. Hiller, a rather formal but friendly man who wore a dramatic mustache, had come into Grosshennig's small gallery carrying a wood frame locket roughly as big around as an apple. The locket held two pieces of glass tightly together, and between them was a lock of hair shaped into a coil.

Hiller explained that his father had placed the hair in the locket years before, when he was still a boy, and after nearly a century of being passed from hand to hand, it now needed some repair. The hair inside it was Beethoven's. He was certain the hair had belonged to the great composer because his father had cut it himself.

Grosshennig felt honored to be given the task of restoring and resealing the locket. When he was finished, the locket was well prepared for many more years of service. The two pieces of glass were clear and polished, and the edges where they touched had been sealed together with glue; Grosshennig had freshly painted the wooden frame and sealed its underside with a covering of brown paper. But the craftsman had done one more thing, he explained to the locket's owner, and he hoped Herr Hiller would not object. Beneath the outer backing was a similar layer of paper on which Grosshennig had written, "Newly pasted to make it dust-free. Original condition improved. Cologne d.18/12 1911." He had signed his name on the paper as well, he explained, because an important relic such as this deserved careful documentation, and also because it meant very much to him to have drawn so near the great composer, even if only briefly and in such a simple manner.

Paul Hiller made his own handwritten inscription on the brown paper that was visible on the locket's underside. The picture framer had been correct, Paul Hiller agreed. It made good sense to document the treasure the locket contained, particularly because the prize the locket held was a bit of the body of Ludwig van Beethoven himself.

Ferdinand Hiller's son, Paul, an opera singer and music journalist, was given the lock of hair by his father in Cologne in 1883, on the occasion of his thirtieth birthday.

Eight

Fleeing the Nazis

*T*wo decades after he refurbished the locket, Paul Hiller, white-haired and handsome, died after suffering a stroke at his home in Cologne in 1934. At his bedside were his wife, Sophie, and his two sons—Edgar, soon to be twenty-eight and an opera singer like his father and grandmother before him had been, and Erwin, then twenty-six and an actor, both sons still living in their parents' home.

A paid obituary appeared in a Cologne newspaper, the small notice bordered in black and headed by a simple Christian cross. "After a life of rich artistic creativity," it read, "righteous up to this death, our unforgettable dear husband and father, Herr Paul Hiller, music writer, passed away unexpectedly. . . . He died firmly believing in his Savior."

Why did Paul Hiller's family choose to note his death in the *Westdeutscher Beobachter*, the Cologne newspaper that was the most fiercely pro-Nazi one at that moment? Did they publish the obituary specifically to mask their Jewish identity, to protect themselves from harassment and the growing threat of violence against Jews? Did that also explain the use of the cross and the short notice's references to Paul Hiller's—and even his family's—devout Christianity?

For four generations the Hildesheim family had called itself Hiller, to help assimilate into middle-class German society as well as to avoid the very real possibility of persecution. Was the posting of Paul Hiller's obituary the continuation of a necessary family lie carried out in frighteningly dangerous times?

⎯⎯>●<⎯⎯

In the months following Paul Hiller's death, it remained unclear precisely how difficult life would become for Germany's Jews, but by the autumn of 1935, the country's Jewish population no longer could vote, nor could Jews hold certain jobs or practice certain professions, and property owned by Jews legally could be seized by the government and given to others. Throughout Germany most Jews began to consider whether it would be wisest to flee their country rather than risk further persecution, and by 1936, when Cologne's streets had become jammed with Nazi soldiers, the city's official address book no longer showed evidence of *any* member of the Hiller family.

Now the mystery of Beethoven's hair would become a part of the hidden history of the events of World War II, because the record of the hair and the Hillers faded into the shadows. Did Sophie Hiller flee Germany for another country where she would be safer? Did her two sons escape as well? Did they travel together, separately, or did they remain in Germany somehow sheltered from view? And what became of the storied lock of Ludwig van Beethoven's hair?

Many questions still remain unanswered, but what is certain is that the lock of hair *did* survive those terrible times. Beethoven's hair reappeared, quite strangely, in the small fishing

Somehow the lock of Beethoven's hair reached the Danish seaport of Gilleleje in October 1943, when thousands of Jews hunted by the Nazis were ferried to safety in Sweden.

port of Gilleleje—pronounced Gill-uh-LIE-uh—on the north coast of the Danish island of Sjælland in October 1943. But how did it reach that small town only a few kilometers across the icy waters of the Øresund from the war-neutral country of Sweden? And where had the lock of hair and the person who kept it safe lived during the years before it turned up in Gilleleje?

Had the lock of hair still remained in Germany on Kristallnacht (the Night of Broken Glass) in November 1938, when German mobs broke the windows of Jewish shops, burned synagogues, and attacked Jewish citizens in the streets of Cologne and throughout all of Germany? How was it that a lock of hair clipped from the head of long-dead Beethoven was one of the few possessions carried by a refugee fleeing for his or her life? And if the lock of hair was carried on the journey simply because it was precious and couldn't be left behind, then why did its owner decide to give it away in Gilleleje on a cold October night?

Nine

Hope for Escape

A member of the Hiller family or someone they knew might have been among the large crowd that gathered at the Copenhagen Synagogue on the morning of September 30, 1943, to hear Rabbi Marcus Melchior make a stunning announcement. He had received a warning that the Germans planned to raid Jewish homes throughout Copenhagen and that all Danish Jews would be arrested and transported to concentration camps.

They know that tomorrow is Rosh Hashanah and our families will be home. The situation is very serious. We must take action immediately. You must leave the synagogue now and contact all relatives, friends, and neighbors you know are Jewish and tell them what I have told you. You must tell them pass the word on to everyone they know is Jewish. You must also speak to all your Christian friends and tell them to warn the Jews. You must do this immediately, within the next few minutes, so that two or three hours from now everyone will know what is happening. By nightfall tonight, we must all be in hiding.

Rabbi Melchior had learned from sympathetic members of the Danish government that Adolf Hitler had ordered the deportation of all Jews in Denmark to begin on October 1. Before nightfall on September 30, a nationwide effort to rescue Denmark's Jews was underway. Messengers were sent from Copenhagen and smaller cities and towns to spread the important news throughout the country. Lutheran ministers made urgent telephone pleas to their parishioners to shelter Jews however they could, and others began to enlist the help of fishermen whose boats would ferry Jews to safety in Sweden.

Taxis and private cars now sped through the Danish countryside toward the fishing villages that lined the Øresund coast, and trains, too, were packed with hushed and frightened passengers wearing as many clothes as they could fit beneath their heavy coats, and carrying as little baggage as possible in order not to arouse suspicion.

The village of Gilleleje on the northern tip of Sjælland soon felt a surge of refugees. On Tuesday, October 5—five days after the rescue effort had begun—the evening train into Gilleleje carried 314 people instead of the three dozen normally on board. But these were not the first refugees to reach Gilleleje. Many others had arrived earlier, had boarded fishing boats docked in Gilleleje's small harbor, and had safely crossed to the port of Höganäs in neutral Sweden, a dozen nautical miles across the wind-chopped water.

Hundreds of frightened Jews eager to follow them to Sweden were now sheltered virtually everywhere in and around the town—in garages and lofts, in sheds and warehouses, at

The church in Gilleleje where Jewish refugees—one of whom carried the lock of Beethoven's hair—hid from the Nazis.

Dr. Kay Fremming was given the lock of hair by one of the desperate Jews hiding in the loft of Gilleleje's church.

the hospital, the boatbuilder's yard, the waterworks, and the brewery. And remarkably, every citizen of Gilleleje—and all of Denmark—who helped hide, feed, and ferry the refugees to Sweden risked arrest, or even death, to do so.

On Wednesday morning, a day that was gray and streaked with rain, a small group of refugees were hiding at the village church. It seemed to make sense to hide a larger group there as well. In an empty loft above the nave, a hundred people or more could be concealed for a long time, if necessary, and soon more refugees arrived at the church. When Reverend Kjeldgaard Jensen, the church's pastor, went to the church door late in the afternoon, he loudly spoke the word *håbe*, "hope," the secret password that proved he was a friend, and then he was let inside. He climbed the steep stairs to the loft and announced to the many people gathered there that he would do everything he could to protect each one of them.

Many other volunteers arrived to help as well, bringing blankets and coats, pots of soup, even a roast to feed the refugees. As soon as night fell, it became too dangerous to turn on even a single light. Buckets were placed in a corner to serve as makeshift toilets, but they could not be located once night fell and the interior of the loft grew dark as a cave. The temperature hovered barely above freezing. People's hands and feet went numb, and the place was eerily silent—more than a hundred people packed into the small attic space, saying nothing for hours on end, not even daring to whisper, the only sound the constant ticking of the clock in the tower, its repetitions seeming to mock the refugees' terrible circumstances.

At some point prior to midnight, Dr. Kay Fremming, one of Gilleleje's two doctors, was called to the church to attend to someone who was ill, and perhaps also to administer sedatives to the youngest children and babies so that they would sleep soundly in the arms of their parents and not cry out and alert the Nazi Gestapo. It is not known how long Dr. Fremming stayed with the refugees in the church loft or whether he still remained when, at about midnight, the Gestapo arrived without warning.

Positioned inside the bolted church door, a man named Arne Kleven, who was helping to protect the refugees, heard shouted words in German and pounding on the door with a rifle butt. For nearly two hours he refused to open the door despite the loud demands of Gestapo Chief Hans Juhl that he and his men be allowed inside. Then Juhl announced that he was prepared to firebomb the building. The refugees and those who were protecting them would either be forced out by the smoke, or they would all burn to death, or they could spare themselves and open the door and surrender. It was their decision, he shouted.

At 5:00 a.m., Arne Kleven took a deep breath, steeled himself for whatever was about to follow, and opened the heavy door. People in the loft above him had begun to plead for him to do so, and he, too, knew that hope now was utterly lost. Seconds later, soldiers armed with machine guns bounded into the loft, aimed blinding lights on the huddled, frozen figures they found there, and forced them all out of the loft and into the night. Then they were loaded into canvas-topped troop trucks bound for the Horserød prison camp near Helsingør. Although hundreds of others had successfully escaped, the one hundred twenty Jews hidden in the church loft that night had failed in their desperate effort to reach exile in Sweden.

We do not know precisely when, or where, someone fleeing for his or her life gave Dr. Kay Fremming a coiled knot of Ludwig van Beethoven's hair held in a wood frame locket. The identity of that person may remain a mystery forever. Although there were rumors in the small harbor town for months, even years, afterward that Dr. Fremming had been given something very precious by one of the hunted refugees, he was a quiet man who never spoke openly about the lock of Beethoven's hair.

There are clues with which it is possible to piece together an idea of how the gift might have been made. Marta Fremming, the doctor's wife, confirmed before her death that the lock of hair was given to her husband in the midst of those dramatic days of the rescue of the Jews, but she offered no fuller explanation other than to acknowledge that she and her husband were active in the collective effort to protect the Jews who came to their town in hopes that they could find a way to freedom in Sweden.

Was the hair an offering of gratitude for medical assistance Dr. Fremming gave, or simply someone else's keepsake he agreed to hold until the day when its owner could return for it? These questions remain unanswered, but what is absolutely certain is that this fragile bit of the real Beethoven was placed into Dr. Kay Fremming's possession during those days of heroism on Denmark's shore.

The Gilleleje church was never again used as a hiding place. But in the end, the people of the town were stunningly successful in their efforts to help the country's Jews reach safety.

More than 1,300 refugees successfully found their way to freedom in Sweden via that single harbor town, far more than from any other village on the Danish coast. Nationwide a total of 7,906 people were escorted safely to Sweden's shores in the autumn of 1943. Only 580 failed to escape.

Jews escaped Denmark because the nation's leaders and citizens heroically agreed that they *would* escape, and they worked bravely toward that end in October 1943, believing that the Nazi horror simply could not be allowed to succeed in their beloved homeland. Given what we know of Beethoven's love of humanity, his concern about human rights, and his passion for life, it is fitting that something of him was present in that historic moment, when the right thing was done in the midst of a very dark time.

Ten

Hair for Sale

*O*n the morning of May 5, 1945, listeners in Denmark whose radios were tuned to the BBC in England heard the fantastic news that the German forces had surrendered. At last Danes were in control of their country again. The lives of almost all Danish citizens—Jews and non-Jews alike—had been spared during the war, and they now were overjoyed that it was over.

Throughout the rest of Europe, most of those Jews who were not killed had nothing to return to—their homes and businesses had been seized, everything they owned had been taken by others, and their previous lives no longer existed. But in Copenhagen and throughout Denmark, many of the Jewish refugees who had spent the last years of the war in Sweden returned home to find their houses and apartments secure and clean, their kitchens freshly stocked with food as a welcome from their neighbors, their jobs and their businesses awaiting their safe return.

Orphaned children from European countries that had been devastated by the war began to arrive in Denmark as well. Early in 1946 a group of French war orphans made the journey north and were matched with families eager to adopt them. Among the group who were sent to the town of Gilleleje was a six-year-old girl from the village of Sannois near Paris named Michele de Rybel. Although she knew nothing of Beethoven at the time, she later played a key role in the story of what happened to his hair.

Michele had been frightened about what was in store for her when she was put aboard a train in Paris bound for Copenhagen, carrying only a single small suitcase containing a few remnants of the life she had known before the war. She was delighted to discover that the town that was her destination lay beside a beautiful sea, but when she arrived in Gilleleje she was disoriented by a language that sounded like nothing she had ever heard. And the county administrator and his wife who were supposed to be her new parents were unkind to her.

After three months with her adoptive parents, Michele was healthy, yet she was bitterly homesick and hated her new life. She knew that at six years of age she could not manage to find her way back to France, but perhaps she *could* find other people in Gilleleje who would treat her like a true daughter.

The doctor and his wife, the nurse, had been very kind to her when she had visited their clinic for an examination, and when she discovered that they had no children of their own, she simply sat down in front of their large, yellow-brick house and waited for their return. She had learned enough Danish to be able to say with sincerity, "I want to be *your* daughter."

———×◦×———

It wasn't long before Dr. Kay Fremming, his wife, Marta, and their adopted daughter, Michele, appeared to the townspeople of Gilleleje to be a true family. The three of them enjoyed living in a town that was the kind of community where people worked hard and knew and cared about their neighbors. In winter, after the summer tourists had gone, the town would shrink to a tiny knot of residents who passed those long evenings at home reading, listening to music on Danish Radio as well as on cherished phonograph records, and a few—like Kay with his flute and Marta her cello—even making music themselves. Young Michele began to take music lessons soon after she joined the household, and it was not long before she could play simple duets with her father, who was utterly devoted to her.

Years later, when he retired from his medical practice, Dr. Fremming played the flute in the regional orchestra and collected more than two hundred classical phonograph records—a collection that featured the music of Beethoven.

Eventually Michele completed school, married, and began a family of her own. Then, on a blustery day in late September 1969, her father collapsed on a train that was homeward bound from Copenhagen, where he had gone to buy new phonograph records to add to his collection. Other passengers and the conductor tried to assist him, and an ambulance was waiting at the train's next stop, but at a nearby hospital he could not be revived. Dr. Kay Fremming had died of a sudden and massive heart attack at age sixty-four.

⟫⟪

It was only after her father's death that Michele, whose married name was Michele Wassard Larsen, first heard of the prized lock of Beethoven's hair. It had never even been mentioned in the three decades since she had joined the Fremming family. The hair and the black locket that contained it had simply lain in a drawer in the doctor's desk. Michele's mother explained to her that it had been given to her father by one of the Jewish refugees he helped long ago. She did not know the name of the person who had insisted he take it, but she said her husband had always valued it greatly.

Kay Fremming had been a modest man, Marta reminded her daughter. After the war people had simply moved on with their lives, and no one who had been part of the rescue effort believed he or she had done anything that deserved honor or special remembrance. It wasn't in Kay's nature to take pride in a possession—even one as extraordinary as Beethoven's hair.

In the years after her father's death, Michele and her mother seldom spoke of the lock of hair again. It continued to lie in a desk drawer until the mid-1970s, when Marta decided to make a gift of the lock of hair to her daughter. For the first time in at least forty years, the lock of hair saw the light of day as it hung on a wall in Michele's home.

Then Michele's husband, Ole, just thirty-eight at the time, suffered a sudden heart attack and died. Not yet forty and already widowed, Michele now had to struggle to support two young sons by herself. She accepted a position at the library in the town of Holte, and she and her sons managed as best they could. By the time her mother, Marta, almost eighty-six, entered a nursing home in 1994—her body weak and frail, her memory entirely gone—Michele had seen the boys through school and into adulthood. And it was with her younger son, Thomas, that Michele first began to discuss the possibility of selling the lock of hair she was amazed that she possessed.

Yes, the black-framed locket with the coil of hair inside was a memento of her father, and a reminder of a time when he and his neighbors had refused to allow the Nazis to carry out their madness in Denmark, but she and Thomas finally concluded that if the lock of hair did have real monetary value, perhaps it would be best for her to sell it. At the Copenhagen office of Sotheby's, the international auction house through which many artworks and antiques are sold, the shy and petite

Michele Wassard Larsen and her son Thomas Larsen. After the lock of hair had remained in their family for more than fifty years, they chose to sell it in an auction at Sotheby's in London.

woman with short-cropped, silver hair and her tall and striking son arrived to inquire about the possibility of selling the hair.

It was common for Sotheby's to receive inquiries about any number of supposedly rare and precious objects. But although the manager was initially skeptical about how a Danish library employee like Michele might have come to possess a relic of the master composer, the potential for this to actually be his hair was intriguing. Experts at the company's offices in London would need to examine the locket and the lock of hair it contained to determine its authenticity, of course, but perhaps it really *was* Beethoven's hair.

Within little more than a week, the head of Sotheby's Books and Manuscripts Department expressed confidence that the lock of hair had indeed been cut from the head of Ludwig van Beethoven, and that the company would agree to sell it on Michele's behalf at its next "music and continental books" auction, scheduled for December. Sotheby's was willing to vouch for the hair's authenticity for a number of reasons. The locket's wooden frame was consistent with those that were common in Germany early in the nineteenth century; its paper backing and inscription appeared never to have been tampered with; Ferdinand Hiller indeed had a son named Paul who would have been thirty years old on May 1, 1883, as the note claimed, and, most critically important, it was well-documented that Ferdinand Hiller had made several visits to the dying composer and had remained in Vienna until after Beethoven's funeral.

On May 26, 1994, Michele signed a simple contract allowing the London house to sell at auction "1 lock of hair (framed) from Beethoven. Given as a present to Paul Hiller, whose father did the cutting of the hair 27 March 1827."

———◦———

In London on the rainy morning of December 1, 1994, an agent and rare-music dealer paid particular attention as an auctioneer opened the brisk bidding on the lock of Beethoven's hair. In the matter of only a few moments he had purchased it for clients in the United States whose names were not revealed. A letter notifying Michele of the successful sale was mailed the following morning, and she was both saddened and very pleased by the news. The money it would bring to her would be helpful, but the small oval locket had been part of the lives of her family for a long time. Although she hadn't known about it at the time, it had been a part of her life from the day she stubbornly sat down on the steps in front of a yellow-brick house in Gilleleje to claim a family for herself.

Eleven

Beethoven: Ode to Joy

*B*eethoven never married and never had children of his own, but when his brother Caspar Carl died in November 1815, leaving a will that named the composer as the guardian of his young son, Karl, Beethoven took the responsibility very seriously. The boy's mother, Joanna, with whom Beethoven always had quarreled, was named co-guardian, but Beethoven was determined to raise the boy alone. For nearly five years he fought a bitter court battle with Joanna for sole custody of Karl. The boy did live solely with Beethoven for a time, but ran away to live with his mother and said he was happier with her.

By the time Beethoven ultimately won by asking powerful friends to intervene with the court, the long fight had kept him from composing music daily for the first time in his life, and the emotional conflict and his bad health had aged him terribly. The court ruled that Karl, now thirteen, had to live with his uncle, and they would be primary family to each other from now on.

Beethoven often appeared in public looking as if whole weeks had passed without his bathing or changing his clothes, yet he was, nonetheless, as professionally distinguished as anyone in Vienna. His huge talents had brought him uncommon renown, but still he did not have the private life he longed for. Beethoven wanted a secure and nurturing home life, but his nephew Karl felt he had been taken away from his mother for no good reason. Beethoven wanted to love and be loved in return, but although he tried unsuccessfully to marry several times, his difficult temperament continued to make this impossible. His moodiness was constant and his angry eruptions created many enemies; he fought with landlords, he and Karl moved often, and he was almost always ill now. Yet much work—and much misery—remained ahead for him.

Beethoven was stricken with jaundice, the yellowing of the skin that signaled liver disease, followed by more terrible stomach pain that kept him in bed for weeks. Then in 1823, a year in which he hoped he could focus on making progress on a new symphony, he was attacked by still more abdominal troubles, by a severe respiratory infection that would not go away, and by an utterly new disorder, this time piercing pain in his eyes that was made worse by bright light.

It had been a decade since music-mad Vienna had hosted the premiere of a major orchestral work by Beethoven, and four years had passed since he made his final appearance at a concert podium—conducting his Seventh Symphony but hearing it not at all. So it was with great anticipation that a gala concert was scheduled at Vienna's Kärntnertor Theater in May 1824, one that would include, as the announcement proclaimed, "A Grand Symphony with Solo and Chorus Voices entering in the finale on Schiller's poem Ode to Joy."

Setting the poem to music had been a dream of Beethoven's since he was a young man. The idea in the poem of a loving Father dwelling above a world at peace was powerful to Beethoven, and the response to Beethoven's new music by those in attendance on that spring evening was more than he could have hoped for. The concert hall was packed. Beethoven had gone so far as to dress up, wearing a dark green frock coat, white neckerchief and waistcoat, black silk breeches and stockings, and shoes with brass buckles, his thick head of graying hair carefully combed and pinned back for the occasion. But because he could not hear, his only task was to stand near the conductor and set the tempo of each of his new symphony's movements.

When the timpani drums thundered in the second movement, the audience broke out into spontaneous applause, then did so four more times. A brilliant fanfare concluded the fourth movement of the symphony before a single bass voice rang out in German, "O Friends, no more these sounds! Let us sing more cheerful songs, more full of joy!" And then the entire chorus joined the singer, their hymn sung to hope and brotherhood: "You millions, I embrace you. This kiss is for all the world!"

At the symphony's conclusion, applause and shouted cheers rose throughout the concert hall, but Beethoven simply stood at his music stand, unaware of the response until one of the soloists took him by the arm and turned him toward the audience so at least he could see the overwhelming response of the people whom his symphony had so enthralled. His face remained expressionless as he peered out at them, and as they cheered, he offered a simple bow—the final time he would ever stand on a stage and acknowledge the public's praise. When he bent slightly at the waist, the applause and cries grew louder still, white handkerchiefs waved like flags from hundreds of hands, and a hundred hats sailed into the air in celebration of the masterwork.

Twelve

Two Americans with a Dream

*I*ra Brilliant returned to the United States after serving in World War II, married his sweetheart, Irma, and had a daughter, Maxine. Although Maxine was developmentally disabled, she learned to play the piano by the time she was ten—exhibiting remarkable musical talent—but then she suddenly died. When Ira listened to the Beethoven sonata titled *Les Adieux*, it seemed to express the loss of someone beloved—and it reminded him of his daughter.

The terrible pain the Brilliants felt in Maxine's absence led them to sell their New York business, load their possessions in a station wagon, and drive west with their seven-year-old son, Robert, until they reached sunny Arizona and a fresh start. Ira found work selling real estate and investing in land in Phoenix, and in a decade, he had thrived in ways he never imagined, achieving enough financial success that he set out to collect things the great Beethoven had touched or created.

He was powerfully drawn to specific passages of Beethoven's music, and was also fascinated by the way in which Beethoven had been able to compose such extraordinary music despite his difficult life and deafness. Ira carefully began to turn his passion for Beethoven's music into something tangible and lasting.

The young man whose friends called him "Che" grew up in Laredo, Texas, in the 1950s on the U.S. side of the shallow Rio Grande, the river that forms the border with Mexico. His mother was a native of the Mexican state of Nuevo León, and his father held a series of jobs managing gas stations in Laredo's barrios, businesses where Che was required to work beginning when he was ten.

He had grown up speaking Spanish in the small, single-room cinder block house his father had built, and once in school, he learned English effortlessly and soon proved to be an excellent student. By the time he reached high school, he had read every volume of the World Book encyclopedia simply because he enjoyed its wide range of subjects. The high school science project to which he had devoted himself for three years earned him awards at both national and international science fair competitions and provided entrance to Northwestern University near Chicago.

It was in college in 1970 that Che had first become intrigued by classical music, and although he was a passionate Beatles fan, before long the music he most wanted to hear was Beethoven's. By the time he entered medical school, Che Guevara knew he wanted to listen to Beethoven's music forever, but he didn't know yet what a powerful connection he would share with the famous composer.

After Che completed his training as a urological surgeon, he opened a practice in Nogales, Arizona, a town on the Mexican border where his wife, Reneé, had been raised. The couple had three sons, and Che was a long way from being the affluent physician he dreamed of becoming back when he was five years old and almost always hungry. But as he worked overtime, his medical practice succeeded and he built a fine new medical clinic. Che felt the new space was a perfect one in which he could host an annual birthday party in Beethoven's honor. He served an elaborate Mexican buffet, beautifully costumed mariachis serenaded the guests, and a bright banner that ringed the waiting room read "Happy Birthday, Ludwig van Beethoven."

Che and Ira met for the first time when he invited the Brilliants to come to Nogales to join the celebration in December 1993. Mutual friends had assured the doctor that Ira Brilliant was as passionate about Beethoven as he was, and when they met, the two men discovered that, although they were very different people, both held the composer in higher esteem than virtually anything else in their lives.

By now Ira had become a serious collector of Beethoven letters, musical scores, and first editions of his compositions, and Che found himself increasingly intrigued by the way in which Ira had been able to bring Beethoven to life for many people by gathering together scattered mementos from the time long ago when the master had made his powerful music. Although Dr. Guevara felt he could not afford to make expensive purchases, he told his new friend he would love to possess *something*, some token of Beethoven and his times.

In all his years of collecting, Ira never had been able to acquire a fine first edition of Beethoven's first published composition, his Opus 1, the Piano Trios nos. 1–3. It was a rare and expensive document, and Ira kept hoping to find it offered for sale so he could add it to the collection of the Center for Beethoven Studies. In early November 1994 good fortune seemed to arrive in the mail. In the Sotheby's catalog Ira spotted precisely what he had been looking for. To be sold in London on December 1 was a first edition Opus 1 in excellent condition.

But there was something else in the catalog that also quickly caught his eye. In the two decades since he had become a collector, he never had encountered human remains of any kind

22

33

√31 BEETHOVEN (LUDWIG VAN) GRANDE FUGUE tantôt libre, tantôt recherchée pour 2 Violons, Alte & Violoncelle...Oeuvre 133, FIRST EDITION OF THE GROSSE FUGE, complete parts, 10,9,9 and 9 pages, engraved throughout, plate number 877, a little light staining, otherwise in good condition, Vienna, Math. Artaria, [1827]

RARE. Although given a separate opus number 133, the "Grosse Fuge" was in fact originally composed as the final movement of the String Quartet in B flat major Op.130. See previous lot.

Bought Jn £1,500-2,000

√32 BEETHOVEN (LUDWIG VAN) FIDELIO Drame lyrique en deux actes, [full score], 2 volumes, 535 pages, engraved music, plate number M.S.2033, contemporary half roan, folio, Paris, Maurice Schlesinger, [c.1836]; with Sir Henry Wood's copy of Weingartner's arrangement of the "Grosse Fuge", a first edition of Bizet's arrangement of Saint-Saëns's "Introduction et Rondo Capriccioso" and another—Blainville (Charles Henri) Histoire générale, critique et philologique de la musique, FIRST EDITION, lacking frontispiece and about eight other plates (as often), contemporary calf, rebacked, [Hirsch, Anhang 6], 4to, Paris Pissot, 1767; and one other, sold as a collection not subject to return (7)

Bought Jn £400-500

√33 BEETHOVEN (LUDWIG VAN) LOCK OF BEETHOVEN'S HAIR, with autograph note of authentication signed by Paul Hiller, son of Ferdinand Hiller, who took the cutting ("Diese Haare hat meine Vater Dr. Ferdinand v. Hiller am Tage nach Ludwig van Beethovens Tode, d.i. am 27. März 1827, von Beethoven's Leiche abgeschnitten und mir...übergeben. Côln, am 1. Mai 1883. Paul Hiller"), framed and glazed, oval, c.10.5 x 9.5cms.

The fifteen-year old Ferdinand Hiller was taken to see Beethoven by Hummel; he recorded his visits in "Aus dem Tonleben unserer Zeit" (1871: see Thayer, pp.1044ff).

£3,600   Caster + Dr Guevara purchase £2,000-3,000

√34 BEETHOVEN (NIKOLAUS JOHANN VAN, 1776-1848, younger brother of the composer) AUTOGRAPH LETTER SIGNED ("v.Beethoven[paraph]"), to Frau von Vilguth in Linz, thanking her for the remittance of sixty florins to cover the current year's rent, alerting her to his plans to visit Linz and expressing the hope that she is in good health ("...bestättige ich Ihnen den Empfang der mir überschickten f60 auf die heurige Rente vorhienein. Zugleich bemerke ich daß ich bis 17t d. M. von hier gedenke nach Linz zu gehen..."), 1 page, 4to, integral autograph address panel, seal tear slightly affecting a few words, Vienna, 21 June 1842

£500-600

£460

The Sotheby's catalog page listing the locket of hair.

being offered at auction, yet there it was: lot 33, its value estimated in English pounds at £2,000–3,000 and its authenticity certified, a lock of the great Beethoven's hair. Then Brilliant remembered his friend in Nogales.

He was able to reach Che at his clinic at the close of the day, and Ira first reminded his friend that he had asked him to find a suitable Beethoven memento sometime. Yes, of course, the doctor remembered. In that case, the older man posed another question. Would Che by chance be interested in acquiring a bit of Ludwig van Beethoven's hair?

It was a wonderful idea, and Che Guevara enthusiastically agreed to pledge money toward the purchase of the lock of hair. Ira would contribute as well. They didn't know if they would succeed in their effort to buy it, but they most certainly would try. Imagine it, the two men repeatedly said before they ended their phone conversation: a lock of Beethoven's hair.

—>•<—

A fax from London was waiting for Ira Brilliant when he got out of bed on the morning of December 2, 1994, and the news from his agent in London was both bad and good. The Opus 1 score had sold for more than three times the Sotheby's estimate, and almost twice what Ira had authorized him to bid. On the other hand, Macnutt *had* been successful in purchasing the locket of Beethoven's hair. No one had chosen to go beyond the high bid of £3,600, meaning that Guevara and Brilliant would spend a total of about $7,300, once Sotheby's surcharge, the agent's commission, and the shipping charges were tallied.

Brilliant sat down and studied the fax once more, and he could hardly believe what he read. He and Guevara now actually owned a bit of Beethoven. It was truly thrilling to him, but he tried to be calm as he placed an urgent call to Nogales.

"Do you have your comb ready?" he asked when he heard Che Guevara's voice.

As the two men discussed their good fortune, they realized that acquiring the lock of hair also gave them an enormous opportunity, one they were quickly excited by as well. In the desperate and nearly suicidal 1802 letter to his brothers Beethoven had written nearly two hundred years before, he had expressed the hope that one day the reasons for his hearing loss and illnesses might be determined and made public. Beethoven had wanted the world to understand him better. Now perhaps Ira and Che could do something to help fulfill the composer's request at long last. Was *that* the reason, they asked themselves, why the hair so fortuitously and easily had come to them?

Dr. Alfredo "Che" Guevara (left) and Ira Brilliant speaking about their acquisition of Beethoven's hair and the decision to have it scientifically tested.

Thirteen

From Denmark to Arizona

*U*nder normal circumstances it is Sotheby's policy not to disclose the sources of the objects it presents at auction. But on this occasion the head of Sotheby's Books and Manuscripts Department agreed to contact the previous owner of the hair, explaining that the people who now owned it hoped they might learn something of its particular and unlikely journey between the time it was in Vienna to the time when it arrived in Arizona. Sotheby's made it clear to Michele Wassard Larsen in Denmark that she was under no obligation to reveal her identity, nor to describe how the lock of hair had come into her possession. But as it happened, she was very willing indeed.

Two months after the arrival of Beethoven's hair in America, a letter posted from the Danish town of Hillerød and mailed to the Beethoven Center in San José followed it. "Hello!" the typed letter called out in awkward English,

My name is Thomas Wassard Larsen, and i am writing to you about a lock of Beethovens hair, sold by Sotheby's auktions i London. I hope you understand the meening with this letter, because i'm not very good at writing in english.

During w.w.2 . . . my mother was adopted by a nice family in Denmark. . . . My mothers new father was a doctor who helped many of these judes, in the start only with medicin, but later he worked together with the local fishermen, in the night to smuggel judes to Sweden. It was one of these judes who gave the lock of Beethovens hair to him for his help. My grandfather kept this medallion until his dead . . .

Thomas Larsen went on to explain that he and his mother were very pleased that Beethoven's hair had gone to people who greatly appreciated it, who would honor it as they always had. And yes, he said, they would welcome continued communication and would offer whatever help they could in unraveling more of the locket's history.

What the letter conveyed was extraordinary new information for Ira Brilliant. This lock of Ludwig van Beethoven's hair had been a silent witness when Christian Danes helped Jews escape the Nazis, and that truth moved Brilliant in particular. He had fought against the Nazis during the war and was a Jew himself—and soon after the receipt of the letter, he vowed to do everything he could to find any living descendants of Paul Hiller and his father, Ferdinand, the man who had met the mighty Beethoven and who had cut his hair and placed it in a wood frame locket.

Ira felt compelled to learn if, in the aftermath of World War II, any members of the Hiller family had survived in Germany. Had they escaped to other countries to begin their lives again? Had they—like the great composer had done— found a way to overcome terrible adversity and go on?

To answer the medical mystery posed by Beethoven's hair, Ira Brilliant and Che Guevara had conversations with scientists as far away as the Massachusetts Institute of Technology and as near at hand as the Lawrence Livermore Nuclear Laboratories, less than an hour's drive from the Beethoven Center in San José, California. Che assembled the team of medical and scientific colleagues who would take the first steps in a process that would require several years to complete. When all the necessary advance work had been finished, a large group of interested people and television crews met at the University of Arizona Medical Center to open the locket that held the precious hair, to see if it might answer some very compelling questions.

Beethoven's tempestuous relationship with his nephew Karl preoccupied him and kept him away from composing music.

Fourteen

Beethoven: The Disgrace

*O*nce he became Karl's official guardian, Beethoven raised his nephew as best he could. At nineteen Karl was eager to please his uncle, but was increasingly plagued by Beethoven's demands, his constant suspicions, and his quick anger. Karl complained to his friends that he was growing tired of the ongoing conflict with his uncle, and that he wanted a life that was very different from what Beethoven would approve.

Beethoven disliked Karl's friends and was mistrustful of their motives, and he disapproved of Karl's determination to join the army. Beethoven would simply not allow it. He complained that the boy was lazy, and he was outraged that Karl secretly continued to see his mother. For his part, Karl explained, "I grew worse because my uncle wanted me to be better."

Tensions between them escalated, and then in July 1826, as Beethoven was at work on a new string quartet, he received shocking news.

"Do you know what has happened? My Karl has shot himself!" Beethoven announced to a friend he encountered in the street. "It was a glancing shot; he is still living, there's hope that he can be saved—but the disgrace he has brought upon me; and I loved him so." It was typical of him that Beethoven considered the horrible event's effect on his reputation as quickly as he worried about his nephew's survival from a suicide attempt, but there was no doubt that Karl's action devastated the composer.

Karl's skull was wounded by a bullet in his suicide attempt, and it was some time before he was released from the hospital. Beethoven ultimately agreed to allow him to join the army and, as a peace offering, even suggested that his nephew should spend a bit of time with his mother. And in October Karl, who was still recovering from his wound, came to stay with Beethoven, and Beethoven's only living brother, Johann, at a farm in the country.

Beethoven loved being in the farmlands again and enjoyed spending time with his family. He completed work on the new string quartet, unaware that it would be the last finished piece he would ever compose. When he grew ill yet again, he decided it was time for him to return to the city, even though the journey would be very difficult.

Fifteen

Science Solves Old Mysteries

The twenty hairs from Beethoven's head arrived at the Health Research Institute in Naperville, Illinois, at the end of May 1996. Dr. William Walsh, who directed the institute and was the nation's leading hair researcher, led the investigations with the help of other scientists. Walsh proceeded cautiously, focusing his work in two areas. Trace-metal analysis, done with very sophisticated microscopes, searched for abnormal concentrations of an array of metals that might be contained in the hair. And DNA testing could provide insight into genetic disorders the composer might have suffered from birth, as well as make possible future comparisons with other known Beethoven remains, like other locks of hair, and bone fragments from his skull that had not been reburied when Beethoven's body had been exhumed and moved to another location.

Walsh did not perform the testing himself, but instead selected a group of scientists whom he believed were the best in their areas of expertise. Each scientist was told only that he or she was examining the hair of a "famous person," and Walsh allowed each one to proceed with his experiment only after he was convinced of the soundness of each scientist's plan. All work was performed free of charge, and Walsh and the owners of the hair agreed to be very patient while each test was undertaken. The testing of the hair would be done by scientists who were obligated to fulfill many other investigations and who would have to work it into their busy schedules. Two and a half years passed before at last Walsh flew to Phoenix and presented Che Guevara and Ira Brilliant with a preliminary report of the findings he and the scientists had obtained. The report greatly surprised the two men who had acquired Beethoven's hair.

Walsh had determined that the best person to look for trace metals in the hair was Walter McCrone, the founder of the McCrone Research Institute in nearby Chicago and the foremost microscopist in the U.S. It was McCrone who had demonstrated conclusively in the 1970s that the outline of a figure on fabric known as the Shroud of Turin had been painted in the fourteenth century and was not, therefore, the burial cloth of Jesus, as some had claimed, but was an historic hoax instead. Prior to that determination, McCrone had also proven—by examining another sample of historically important hair—that Napoleon had not died from arsenic poisoning, as long had been rumored.

In his examination of two of the Beethoven hairs, McCrone had first incinerated each one in what is called a low-temperature nascent oxygen asher. The ash from Beethoven's hair, and that of three more hairs taken from living people as a control group, were then scanned using a sophisticated electron microscope. This type of microscope uses nuclear reactions and quantum physics rather than light and magnification in order to "peer inside" a test material. Walsh explained that the "evaluation of trace elements in hair can be quite complex, and requires knowledge of metal metabolism, nutrient transport, excretion kinetics, bile shunting, and many other biochemical processes and factors."

What the scientist found by breaking down and examining the hair at the atomic level was truly surprising. The three control samples contained normal levels of each of the forty-one elements the scientist expected to find in a hair sample. The Beethoven samples were normal as well, with one stunning exception. The Beethoven hair contained an average of *forty-two times* more lead than the control samples did.

McCrone passed his findings on to Walsh, and Walsh included them in the report he presented in person to Ira Brilliant and Che Guevara. Ludwig van Beethoven, Walsh now believed strongly, had been massively poisoned by lead at the time of his death and may have been for decades before. Beethoven's hair had revealed a secret no one had previously known and one that could explain a great deal about the health problems that plagued his life and eventually caused his death.

One of the greatest musicians the world has ever known, Beethoven achieved great acclaim despite terrible physical hardships.

Sixteen

The Unknowable Secrets
of History

*I*ra Brilliant was fascinated by the scientific inquiry into Beethoven's hair, but that was only half of the mystery it held. Tracing the hair's trip through time was equally fascinating to him. What had become of the descendants of the hair's original owner? It is very difficult to trace individual people and objects in times of war and genocide. But Brilliant had resolved not only to safeguard the hair but also to meet the moral responsibility of trying to find living descendants of Paul Hiller, if he could.

Ira now presumed that Paul's widow, Sophie Hiller, or one of her two sons had fled north to Denmark, taking the locket that contained Beethoven's hair with them. But the townspeople of Gilleleje had known the names of virtually none of the refugees who passed through on their way to Sweden during the dramatic rescue. So, would it ever be possible to prove who had pressed the locket of hair into Dr. Kay Fremming's hands?

⇒◦⇐

Each new possibility that Ira Brilliant pursued proved to be a dead end, and it wasn't until Michele Wassard Larsen and her son Thomas took up the search themselves that finally a few leads began to emerge, clues that pointed to the moment when someone had given Beethoven's hair to her father, the doctor.

Danish professor Christian Tortzen's book, *Gilleleje, Oktober 1943*, describes how Danish opera singer Henry Skjær had taken an active role in the Jewish rescue effort in the seaside town. Tortzen had been told by one of the refugees that it was Skjær himself who had personally directed her and her family to the Gilleleje church, and many people remembered that he had been very much involved in efforts to help Jews escape. That information at last connected the musical world in which Paul Hiller's family had been at home in Cologne and the appearance of a lock of Beethoven's hair in a far distant Danish fishing village.

Skjær owned a vacation home near Gilleleje, and he had temporarily housed about forty refugees in that home before they were transferred to the church loft. No one knew whether one or more of those people was named Hiller, however. Yet because of a possible opera connection between the Hiller family and Henry Skjær, surely it made sense to suspect that Edgar Hiller, son of Paul Hiller and an opera singer, had been one of those refugees.

It seemed to Michele Wassard Larsen in Denmark, as well as to Ira Brilliant far away in Phoenix, that at last the pieces of the puzzle were falling into place. Surely Edgar Hiller would have taken the lock of Beethoven's hair with him if he had fled to Denmark. It was also reasonable to assume that his musical colleague Henry Skjær would do everything possible to help him escape. Edgar Hiller could have given the hair to Dr. Fremming himself as he tried to escape to Sweden, or he might have given it to someone else who had passed it to the doctor.

Everything fit together perfectly except for a single troublesome fact. At the massive Danish national archives in Copenhagen, there was no evidence that Edgar Hiller or anyone in his family had ever been in the country. The names of thousands of German Jews who had entered Denmark—legally and illegally as well—during the 1930s and 1940s, including two dozen or so named Hiller, had been carefully catalogued, and each individual's date of birth and the city he or she had come from was recorded as well. But the birth dates and home cities of none of the immigrants named Hiller came close to matching those of Paul Hiller's wife or his two sons. The names Sophie, Edgar, or Erwin Hiller simply did not appear in the archive. What had happened to them?

A researcher at the Yad Vashem in Israel reported that the museum's huge database showed no evidence that Sophie

Hiller, Edgar Hiller, or Erwin Hiller had died at the hands of the Nazis between the years 1935 and 1945. These records were not comprehensive—many people had died and not been accounted for, but the Nazis had kept meticulous records of the men, women, and children who were transported to concentration camps, and most of those records had been carefully preserved after the war.

The sole sign of the Hiller family that the Israeli researcher was able to uncover was a Red Cross Tracing Service document that made it appear very likely that a German Jew named Erwin Hiller, born in 1908, had sailed to New York on June 16, 1948. This small bit of information appeared to be another potential breakthrough. If Erwin Hiller had immigrated to America, then surely he or his descendants could be located. He would be ninety by now and he *might* still be alive. Surely his children would be—if he had any.

But after months of searching for evidence of him, it seemed as if Erwin Hiller had simply vanished the moment he stepped off the SS *Marine Flasher* and onto a New York City pier. Extensive searches at a number of agencies all turned up nothing. Paul Hiller's son Erwin, an actor in Cologne when his whereabouts became unknown following his father's death, had clearly come to America, only to disappear a second time. But then Ira Brilliant discovered records that showed Edgar Hiller had died in Hamburg on November 20, 1959, that he had never married and had had no children, and that his small estate had been willed to his brother, who lived in Los Angeles,

California, and whose name, strangely, was "Marcel Hillaire."

It was amazing news to the knot of people on two continents who had been searching for Paul Hiller's sons as a part of the mystery of what had happened to Beethoven's hair. The American who called himself Marcel Hillaire claimed that he had been born in Cologne on April 23, 1908, just as Erwin Hiller had. He had sailed to America from Germany on June 16, 1948, and that date matched Erwin Hiller's emigration record as well. He lived in New York City, working as a Broadway and television actor, until 1954, when he moved to Los Angeles to establish his

Erwin Hiller became the "French" actor Marcel Hillaire when he immigrated to the United States after World War II. Here he appears as a French chef in the film Sabrina, *which starred Audrey Hepburn.*

film career. He lived in California until his death on January 1, 1988, when he died from complications following surgery.

Like his brother Edgar, Erwin—now Marcel—never married and he did not have any children. But his death certificate had been signed by a woman named Esther Taylor, who continued to live at the same Burbank, California, address where she had lived eleven years before.

For years Ira Brilliant had hoped that one day he could meet one of Paul Hiller's descendants and create a living connection to the historic relic of Beethoven's hair. Although Esther Taylor was not a blood relation of the man whose name had become Marcel Hillaire, she had become his heir, so that would be as close as Ira would come.

Esther Taylor was amazed when her telephone rang one day in 1999, and she began to reply to a series of unexpected questions. Yes, she said, Marcel Hillaire had been her dear friend until his death. Yes, he had been born under the name Erwin Hiller and had been raised in Cologne. He had changed his name and adopted the accent and false history of a Frenchman in order to make a fresh start in the United States after the war. He thought his history—plus the fact that he had a German accent—would prevent him from getting acting work, but that with a French identity he could succeed. Yes, his father had been Paul Hiller, the German music journalist, and yes, of course, Marcel had told her many times about the lock of hair his father possessed, one that his grandfather had cut from the corpse of the great Beethoven.

Seventeen

Remaining Mysteries &
Important Answers

*E*sther Taylor knew that a lock of Beethoven's hair had been in her dear friend's family for two generations, but she could not explain how it had reached Denmark, nor could she name the person who had given it to Dr. Fremming.

Esther had been a pulmonary therapist working at Brotman Memorial Hospital in Los Angeles when she met Marcel Hillaire in the spring of 1974, just days after he was hit by a speeding automobile as he attempted to cross a busy street. His injuries were extensive and he had been hospitalized for months. Despite the four decades that separated their ages, the two grew very close, and when at last he was released from the hospital, Esther Taylor and Marcel Hillaire found an apartment in Los Angeles and lived together for the next eight years. Esther knew her friend would have been hugely helpful in explaining how the lock of hair had left his family and traveled to Denmark if he had remained alive.

Did the person who ultimately gave the hair to Dr. Fremming know precisely where it had come from, or had the black locket with the bit of Beethoven inside been passed from hand to hand several times before it reached the town of Gilleleje?

⟶◆⟵

The scientific analysis of the hair continued, and Che Guevara and Ira Brilliant were thrilled that critically important new information about the cause of the composer's many physical problems was coming to light. The symptoms of lead poisoning, a condition physicians call plumbism, read like a list of Beethoven's lifelong ailments. Ingestion of large amounts of lead almost always causes severe abdominal cramping, vomiting, constipation, and diarrhea. Gout is common, as is joint pain, recurring headaches, loss of appetite, irritability, forgetfulness, and strange and erratic behavior, as well as a kind of clumsiness caused by the partial paralysis of muscles in the arms and legs. Other symptoms that are widely acknowledged in the medical literature, but which are less common, are eye problems and the loss of hearing caused by permanent damage to the optic and auditory nerves.

The very high lead levels that Walter McCrone had detected in Beethoven's hair indicated only the fact that Beethoven was massively poisoned by lead in the last months of his life. Yet given his thirty years of mounting illnesses, his foul moods and emotional problems, and his documented clumsiness, it now appeared very likely that Beethoven had consumed large amounts of lead long before the time of his last illness and his death.

Is it possible that in 1795 or thereabouts, Beethoven somehow ingested a massive quantity of lead in a single dose? Perhaps he had drunk lead-tainted water in large quantities at a spa where he had retreated to attend to his poor health. The dangers of lead were not known at the time, so Beethoven would not have been intentionally poisoned by anyone. In Beethoven's day lead was commonly found in many household objects. He could have been exposed to lead daily as he used dishes with lead glazes, or mugs, cups, pots, and pans made with lead. But because many other people used the same sorts of lead-tainted objects, why didn't a number of them share his symptoms? Beethoven may have been poisoned by the same source of lead repeatedly throughout his life, or from a combination of sources.

Beethoven drank lots of wine, which in those days was often "plumbed" with lead to make it taste less bitter. And there is also one more possible culprit as a source for large amounts of lead. Beethoven saw dozens of doctors over the years, some of the best in Europe and also many who had little or no real medical training. Many of these unskilled "barber surgeons" commonly prescribed lead pills for a wide variety of illnesses. It is entirely possible that throughout his life Beethoven was poisoned by the very "medication" he took to try to improve his terrible health, and that as each illness was treated, his health cascaded down into more serious symptoms of lead poisoning.

⸻⸻

William Walsh, Ira Brilliant, and Che Guevara agreed that it probably would be impossible to ever positively identify what had caused the lead in Beethoven's hair to exceed forty times the normal levels. And Walsh was now eager to test other Beethoven remains to see if lead amounts were similarly high in them. He knew that testing the bone remains of Beethoven would verify the results of the hair analysis and would also show that lead was present in Beethoven's body for much longer than the months it took for his hair to grow to the length of the lock.

If hair and bone were then compared by DNA sequencing and found to have come from the same human being, Walsh, Guevara, and Brilliant could make an airtight case for the accuracy of the testing of the hair, and chronic lead poisoning would explain the composer's medical history and perhaps even the cause of his deafness and death.

Two Vienna physicians had examined small fragments of Beethoven's skull in the mid-1980s in the course of the research for a book they wrote about the composer's diseases. More than a century before, the bones had been acquired in unclear circumstances by a medical history professor who had examined the composer's skeletal remains after his corpse had been exhumed for reburial in Vienna's central cemetery.

The bones had been loaned for the 1980s study by an aging Frenchman, who had inherited them from his great-uncle, that same Vienna professor. Perhaps, just perhaps, the Frenchman who owned the bone fragments could be persuaded to have them examined again.

<hr />

In the summer of 1999, Brilliant, Guevara, and their colleagues succeeded in locating the Beethoven skull fragments that had been studied in Vienna in the 1980s. Their current owner—an American named Paul Kaufmann, the nephew of the

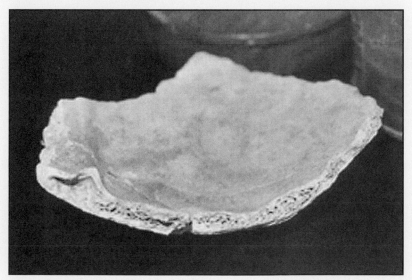

Part of the fragments of Beethoven's skull used for DNA comparison.

Frenchman who had possessed them for many years—agreed to allow the bone to be tested, both to verify the dramatic lead finding in the hair and, via DNA comparison, to determine that both hair and bone had come from the same person.

In September 1999, scientists at Argonne National Laboratories near Chicago, working in collaboration with William Walsh, performed synchrotron X-ray beam experiments on six strands of Beethoven's hair, a control hair with known lead

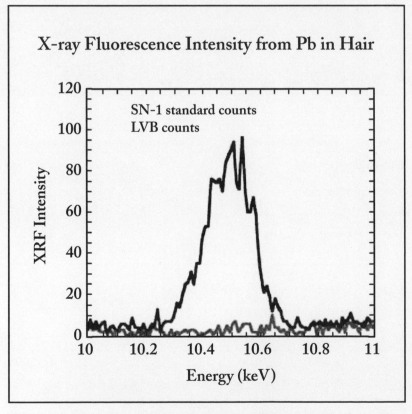

This graph from Argonne National Laboratories demonstrates the shockingly high levels of lead found in Beethoven's hair in comparison with a control sample.

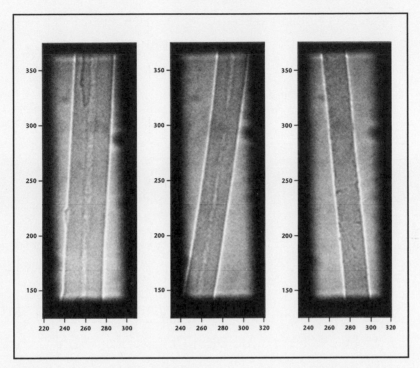

Radiomicrographs of three of Beethoven's hairs shown here are from tests performed at Argonne National Laboratories.

concentration, and a glass film whose lead composition also was already specifically verified.

Because Argonne's Advanced Photon Source is committed for many years in advance to an array of important experiments submitted from all around the world, scientists Ken Kemner, Derrick Mancini, and Francesco DeCarlo had a narrow window of only a few hours on one autumn night to conduct their highly sophisticated experiments on the hair. If they couldn't finish their work within the time allotted, the testing of the hair would have to be postponed, possibly for years.

The micro-imaging techniques used by these scientists were designed to look at the amounts of lead inside the hair and to compare those levels to lead found on the surface of the hair, in order to be sure that the hair hadn't been contaminated by lead *after* Beethoven's death. As the hours and minutes ticked by, the scientists repeatedly ran into problems with the testing, and excitement and frustration grew as they raced against the clock. With only a few minutes remaining for the experiment, they succeeded in focusing an incredibly intense X-ray beam on the six strands of hair, and the pattern danced to life on the computer screen before them. The Argonne team discovered that lead levels in the hair averaged about sixty parts per million, an even higher concentration of lead than had been determined by Dr. McCrone and about ninety times higher than the amount of lead in the contemporary hair sample they also tested.

When the Beethoven skull fragments were subjected to similar testing by the scientists at the Advanced Photon Source, the results also confirmed shockingly high levels of lead in the bone. When lead is ingested it is quickly deposited in bone, where it resides for years, slowly releasing its poison back into the body. Nearly two centuries after his death, it was clear that Beethoven had been exposed to a massive dose of lead, a long-term poisoning by some consistent source of lead, or a cycle of lead exposures that resulted in his lifelong illnesses. Perhaps this diagnosis could even explain something about his deep emotional states and his creative genius.

In the summer of 1999, at about the time the Argonne scientists were performing their first tests on the six strands of Beethoven's hair, DNA scientists at LabCorp in North Carolina were able to determine the genetic fingerprint of strands of Beethoven's hair using a technique known as mitochondrial DNA sequencing. And in the summer of 2005, DNA specialists at the Institute of Legal Medicine at Münster University in Germany examined a piece of Beethoven's skull they were provided by Paul Kaufmann, the fragment's American owner. They were unable to obtain DNA sequencing from bone dust from the fragment, but were able to extract a mitochondrial DNA profile from the bone itself. And the results of the two separate studies—performed on hair and bone in different labs on separate continents—were identical. The two samples had definitely come from the same human being.

It was certain beyond any doubt that the treasured lock that had made such an amazing journey through time and along the way had transformed so many lives was, quite wonderfully, *Beethoven's* hair. As a direct result of the story told by this lock of hair, Beethoven's life would be more completely understood by the generations to follow. It was possible that the emotional power and profound humanity of Beethoven's music had been intensified by his disability and illnesses in even deeper ways than people had previously realized. These results went beyond what Ira Brilliant and Che Guevara had originally dreamed possible—and they had, in fact, completely fulfilled Beethoven's wish.

Eighteen

Beethoven:
The Comedy Is Finished

*B*y 1826 Beethoven's hair had gone quite gray. His physical strength and vitality were gone. His eyes ached; he could hear nothing; and his gut still roiled in pain, surely made worse by the fact that he had begun to drink more wine than ever before.

It was what was called "dropsy," the swelling caused by the retention of fluids, that had begun to plague Beethoven while he stayed with his brother and nephew on his farm in the Austrian countryside. His feet and ankles painfully swelled, then his belly too grew fat with fluid, and by the time he and his nephew Karl began their arduous journey back to Vienna on December 1, he was nearly immobilized by these terrible new symptoms. At home in Vienna Beethoven developed a high fever and a hacking cough, and had a shooting pain in his side. It wasn't until their third day back in the city that Karl was able to secure the services of Dr. Andreas Wawruch, a professor of pathology and clinical medicine at the Vienna Hospital. "One who holds your name in high honor will do everything possible to bring you speedy relief," the physician scribbled into the notebook people used to communicate with Beethoven when the doctor arrived to do what he could for his famous patient.

Beethoven's skin had turned yellow, his breathing was labored, and blood dripped from his mouth. When the doctor visited a second time, he discovered that Beethoven was clearly approaching death. His abdomen had become so swollen that Wawruch now believed there was no choice but to drain its fluid surgically by puncturing Beethoven's abdomen and attaching tubing so the fluid could drain into a large pan. The doctor performed this procedure on December 20, which produced literally gallons of liquid.

Beethoven felt a little better, but only for a short time. He said good-bye to his nephew Karl on January 2, 1827, as the young man left to begin his military posting in Moravia, and the following day Beethoven composed a will making Karl his sole heir. A second tapping on January 8 produced even more liquid than had been drained the first time, and now the poor man was horribly awash in his own fluids, his bedclothes and mattress soaked, a large bowl overflowing beneath his bed, the straw that was meant to protect the floor fouled as well and filled with cockroaches that had been attracted by the stench.

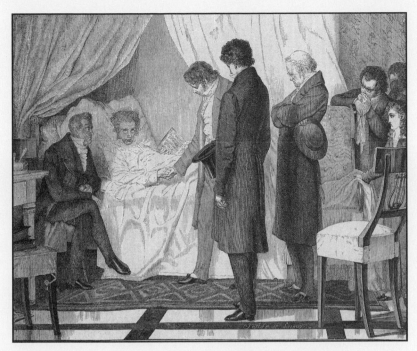

Confined to his bed and in terrible pain, Beethoven continued to sketch musical ideas until the day of his death. Recent tests of his hair proved he took no pain medication, perhaps so he could keep his mind clear for his music.

It was an ugly and undignified way to die. But although the insects disgusted him, Beethoven began to grow calm. He sketched musical ideas and requested favorite food and wine, and he began to receive many visitors, including his old friend Johann Nepomuk Hummel and his fifteen-year-old pupil, Ferdinand Hiller.

Although his spirits were often lifted by the concern people expressed for him, Beethoven's body continued to collapse. Two more abdominal tappings were required in February, and following the fourth, the long-suffering patient now

103

recognized that his time was nearly done. "Applaud, friends, the comedy is finished," he said with a hint of a smile.

Beethoven fell into a coma that endured for two days. Then, in the midst of a late-afternoon snowstorm on March 26, a bright flash of lightning followed by a house-rattling clap of thunder roused him momentarily. He opened his eyes, raised his right hand and clenched it into a fist, then his hand fell back to the bed. Ludwig van Beethoven was dead.

—————————

So many citizens of Vienna were eager to be a part of the funeral proceedings on March 29 that it took ninety minutes for Beethoven's cortège to travel the four blocks from his home to the Trinity Church of the Minorites. At the close of the requiem mass inside the church, his coffin was carried by a hearse hitched to four black horses, and it was followed by as many as two hundred horse-drawn coaches to the parish cemetery, where actor Heinrich Anschütz read a worshipful speech composed for the occasion by beloved Vienna poet Franz Grillparzer. "We who stand here at the grave of the deceased are in a sense the representatives of an entire nation," Anschütz said,

> *The last master of resounding song, the gracious mouth by which music spoke . . . has ceased to be, and we stand weeping over the broken strings of an instrument now stilled.*

Beethoven's Vienna grave. More than 20,000 people crowded into the streets surrounding the Vienna church where his funeral was held on March 29, 1827.

. . . Until his death he preserved a human heart for all men, a father's heart for his own people, the whole world. Thus he was, thus he died, thus will he live for all time!

The bright spring day had gone to dusk when Anschütz's words were finished and it was time to hammer Beethoven's coffin closed and lower it into the earth.

105

Despite his deafness and poor health, Beethoven created 138 major compositions—all of which are still played today—and more than 200 additional minor works.

Afterword

By the time Beethoven died, he had created more than three hundred musical works and set classical music on a bold, modern, and revolutionary new course, one from which it would never turn back. He did so despite heartbreaking personal disappointments, crippling illnesses, and the deafness that ultimately robbed him of the ability to hear his music.

Writing to a lifelong friend, Beethoven described how he coped with his deafness. "I will take fate by the throat; it shall not wholly overcome me. Oh, it would be so lovely to live a thousand lives." The singular and important life he shaped for himself was full of enduring pain and passion. But because he drew magnificent compositions from somewhere deep within him, he continues to reach millions of people around the world.

When the scientific investigations described in the adult book *Beethoven's Hair* were announced, news that Beethoven had been poisoned by lead spread around the world. The book has been translated into twenty-one languages and was made into a documentary film that has been screened at film festivals throughout the world and has aired on television in the United States, the United Kingdom, France, Italy, Australia, New Zealand, Hong Kong, South Korea, Norway, Israel, Finland, Sweden, Germany, and Denmark. Even though hundreds of thousands of people have seen the film and read the book, no new information about the fate of the Hiller family or the person who gave the hair to Dr. Fremming has emerged, and so some of the mysteries of Beethoven's hair remain unsolved, and will, perhaps, forever.

When Ferdinand Hiller clipped the hair as a keepsake in the last days of Beethoven's life, he did so because he believed Beethoven's music already had proven that it would survive through the ages. And in each succeeding era that has followed his death, Beethoven's music has seemed fresh and new and expressive of something essential about the human experience—the truth that there is always suffering in human lives, but that art can transcend suffering in powerful ways.

Notes from the Authors

Writers have as many ways of connecting with interesting stories as there are stories to be told. The inspiration for this book came from a short newspaper article we saw about two Beethoven enthusiasts from Arizona who had purchased a lock of the composer's hair and were about to initiate a series of forensic tests to see what the hair might reveal about Beethoven's life and death.

Clearly there was more to this story. If the testing was successful, what would it reveal? Why were these two men embarking on this unusual quest? What had happened to the hair in all the years between the time it was cut from Beethoven's head and the time they purchased the hair?

Our phone calls to the hair's new owners, Ira Brilliant and Dr. Alfredo "Che" Guevara, were promising, and it was clear that they were fascinating characters in their own right. There was enough material to begin writing a book, with the hope that additional research over the course of a couple of years would prove fruitful.

Discovering more

Beethoven's life has been extensively documented and fact-checked by scholars. Generations of experts have dedicated their professional lives to researching and writing about Beethoven, the creation of his music, the times in which he lived, and the lives of his friends and family. Tens of thousands of pages have been written about these subjects in books and in scholarly journals. We spent many hours poring over these sources so that we would get the details of Beethoven's life right.

The Beethoven-Archiv in Bonn, Germany, offered assistance to this project. We also received help from researchers in Vienna, Paris, London, and Jerusalem. And we worked closely with the Ira F. Brilliant Center for Beethoven Studies and the American Beethoven Society. We recommend that anyone with a passionate interest in Beethoven join the American Beethoven Society, which publishes the *Beethoven Journal*. The society is based at San Jose State University in San Jose, California, and has a chapter in New York City. The Ira F. Brilliant Center for Beethoven Studies is also located at San Jose State University, and we suggest you visit it either in person or online. The center has great educational programs for young people and sponsors concerts and other events throughout the year. It's one of the best places in the world to see materials from Beethoven's life, including the famous lock of Beethoven's hair.

Our biggest challenge in writing this story was the extensive detective work necessary to track the hair through time. Some of the discoveries fell into place as one document led to another, and as one source of information led to a name or date that could be traced. Other breakthroughs took many months to evolve. Genealogists and researchers in Europe and in the United States assisted us. Ira Brilliant and Dr. William Meredith at the Beethoven Center did a great deal of work to track the movements of Beethoven's hair. We were also helped by the Yad Vashem in Jerusalem, which houses many of the documents relating to the Jewish people during the time of the Holocaust.

There are remaining mysteries to be solved. We hope that the publication of this book will generate more discoveries. Perhaps someone who was in Gilleleje during those desperate days in October 1943 will come forward and reveal more about what happened to the hair. Maybe someone is still alive who knows the person who passed the hair to Dr. Fremming. It's possible that someone knows more about what transpired in the church loft, or that someone wrote their recollection of how the hair passed hand-to-hand in a letter or journal entry that hasn't yet been discovered. There may be uncataloged documents from the World War II era that have yet to come to light and that will tell more of the story of what happened to the tiny remnant of the Hiller family. Perhaps a reader of this book will succeed in answering these questions one day.

Crafting the story

The Mysteries of Beethoven's Hair is a bit unusual in that it's based on the stories of a number of people from different eras. The narrative moves from the past to the present in alternating chapters and is also made of two distinct parts. Well-documented information that's a part of the historic record forms one part. The investigation of the hair, which uses the same techniques a detective would apply to solving a case, forms the other. The combination of historical research and new investigation helped shape a book that covered every aspect of what happened to Beethoven's hair.

For those of us built for the telling of stories, there's nothing as exciting as creating one that matters intensely to us, and we hope to others who will enjoy reading it as well. We have both felt a profound connection to Beethoven during the writing of this book. And, like Ira Brilliant and Che Guevara, we have felt responsible to help answer Beethoven's own question about why he suffered so much. We are honored to have told a true story about Beethoven that has helped fulfill his wish that people would understand his struggles and forgive him his shortcomings.

For young writers

If you are curious about becoming a writer, you'll find books to help you learn the craft. But the best thing you can do is to generate many pages of writing to get the feel of it and to find your voice. You'll learn best by doing, and you will grow as an artist over time.

If you're interested in the process of writing a book like *The Mysteries of Beethoven's Hair*, you will note that it is written not in a journalistic style like a typical newspaper article, but in a style known as narrative nonfiction or creative nonfiction. This form requires the writer to stick to well-researched facts, while using the tools of fiction such as plot, voice, scene, character, dialogue, setting, theme, and symbolism to make the telling of a true story as compelling as possible. In this form the writer can't ever make up something and pass it off as being true. And the writer owes it to readers to make it very clear when they are leaving the verifiable and imagining some possibility. Here is an example from chapter three. "Beethoven's father often bullied his son, beating him on occasion, and dragging the crying and frightened boy from his bed to make him practice the piano late into the night." That sentence is based on accounts of his childhood from several sources, including Beethoven himself, and so is reported factually. The next sentence is speculation by the authors, and you'll notice how we communicated this to readers: "It is easy to imagine that his father's rages might have affected the boy's love of music—that the young Beethoven could have turned away from his talent in rebellion against his father—but instead, Beethoven endured the harsh treatment and developed his remarkable talents."

Because narrative nonfiction attempts to be more artful than a piece of research writing, footnotes are not usually included, but you can easily spot the facts in a piece of narrative nonfiction because of the confident way they are presented in the writing. For example, we found the story of Beethoven meeting Mozart in reputable and well-documented historic sources, and so we repeated it in chapter three, because it was reported that Mozart used these very words: "Keep your eye on that one; someday he will give the world plenty to talk about."

We can offer a note of caution about sources of information, which your teachers will no doubt echo. When you write based on research, use only reputable sources of information and be careful about material you find on the Internet, because much of it isn't vetted or verified. A librarian can help guide you to the best and most accurate information on which to base your writing. And if you are relying on recorded interviews of living people as source material for your writing, all the better for you, because you can always go back to those sources with more questions.

If you're curious and want to know more

There are a number of fine biographies about Beethoven for every reading level. A librarian can guide you to just the right books if you'd like to read more.

Many libraries also have a good selection of recordings of Beethoven's music that can be checked out and enjoyed at home. There are Internet sites where you can listen to selections of his music or even full pieces. If you don't know much about Beethoven's music, look up the specific musical works we've mentioned in this book and enjoy listening to the "soundtrack" of *The Mysteries of Beethoven's Hair*. Beethoven's music has proven its power to move generation after generation. And of course, those of you who take music lessons know that Beethoven's music is both a great challenge and an enormous pleasure to play. We hope that learning more about his life will enhance your appreciation of his music.

We have enjoyed working with the interdisciplinary aspects of this story—the way it links the arts, the humanities, and the sciences in interesting ways. If you're interested in the historical eras covered in this book, you can continue to explore the people and times that capture your interest by reading biographies and histories. World War II is a fascinating subject, as is the little-known rescue of the Jews by the Danes. If you're involved in composing or playing music, we hope this book has given you a sense of how one great composer created his music—perhaps it has inspired you to explore other musical lives as well. If you want to learn more about the many branches of science used to study human remains, there are numerous resources for you to pursue. Ask a teacher, a well-read friend, or a librarian to make recommendations. Nothing beats the suggestion of a trusted advisor who has great taste.

Thank you

When the adult version of the story of Beethoven's hair was first published, many young people inquired whether we would create a version of this story especially for them. Thank you to those of you who asked for this book. You spurred us on. Our wonderful grown-up daughter, Megan Nibley, was very supportive, as she always is, and we also received great encouragement from our nephew Alex Nibley, who is a voracious reader. Alex isn't old enough yet to be a Renaissance man—someone who has broad interests and is accomplished in the arts and sciences—but he's clearly a Renaissance boy and a polymath (you can look that word up yourself) who can be trusted to share his honest opinion. Alex was enthusiastic, helpful, and read several drafts. We are pleased to dedicate this book to him, and look forward to being part of his creative life in the years to come.

Our skilled agent, Caryn Wiseman, placed the book with able editors at Charlesbridge. Thank you particularly to Randi Rivers and Harold Underdown. Thanks, too, to the book's designer, Diane Earley, who bridged the life and times of Beethoven and the modern era wonderfully in her design. Thank you to the late Ira F. Brilliant, our friend Alfredo "Che" Guevara, Dr. William Walsh, Esther Taylor, the American Beethoven Society, the renowned Beethoven educator Dr. William Meredith, the Ira F. Brilliant Center for Beethoven Studies, and the center's incomparable curator, Patricia Stroh, who provided invaluable help in sourcing the numerous illustrations in this book. Thank you to the librarians who press this book into just the right hands and to the adults who give this story to the young people in their lives. Our appreciation as well to all of you readers, for letting us tell you the story of what happened to a lock of Beethoven's hair.

Russell Martin and Lydia Nibley
Los Angeles, California

Photo Credits

Jacket
(front, title type): Drawing of Beethoven based on the portrait engraving by Johann Joseph Neidl from 1801. From the collections of the Ira F. Brilliant Center for Beethoven Studies, San Jose State University; (front): Josef Danhauser (1805-1845), Totenmaske [death mask] Ludwig van Beethovens. Fotografie des Ateliers Schaaffhausen. Reproduced by permission from Beethoven-Haus Bonn; (back): The Guevara lock of Beethoven's hair. From the collections of the Ira F. Brilliant Center for Beethoven Studies, San Jose State University.

Casewrap
Silhouette of Beethoven by Joseph Neeson. From the collections of the Ira F. Brilliant Center for Beethoven Studies, San Jose State University.

p. 89: Marcel Hillaire (Erwin Hiller) in *Sabrina*. Reproduced by permission from Esther Taylor and the Estate of Marcel Hillaire.

All of the following photos and illustrations are from the collections of the Ira F. Brilliant Center for Beethoven Studies, San Jose State University and are reproduced with their permission.
pp. i (title type), iii (title type), 10: Drawing of Beethoven, based on the portrait engraving by Johann Joseph Neidl from 1801; p. ii: The Guevara lock of Beethoven's hair; p. vii: Lithograph by Alfred Krause, based on the drawing by August von Kloeber; p. viii: Photo of a painting of Beethoven by Carlo Vestry; p. 2: The Graben in Vienna, steel engraving by I. Owen based on a drawing by Captain Robert Batty; p. 4: Photo of Dr. Alfredo Guevara and Ira Brilliant, Ira holding locket; p. 6: Close-up of Paul Hiller's note from locket; p. 9: The Guevara lock of Beethoven's hair, photograph taken after the locket was opened; p. 13: Beethoven's first meeting with Mozart and the elite of Viennese musical society, based on a painting by August Borckmann; p. 20: Beethoven and Giulietta Guicciardi by Carl Koch; p. 23: Beethoven in the storm by Carl Schweninger; p. 24: Beethoven and the Razumovsky Quartet, based on a painting by August Borckmann; p. 27: Photo of Beethoven's Heiligenstadt apartment; p. 28: Beethoven in the country, based on a painting by Julius Schmid; p. 33: Beethoven's death mask, photograph of the original at the Historical Museum of the City of Vienna; p. 36: Photograph of Ferdinand Hiller by Adolf Halwas; p. 42: Photo of Paul Hiller; p. 45: Photo of Gilleleje harbor; p. 49: Photo of church in Gilleleje, exterior; p. 50: Photo of church in Gilleleje, attic interior; p. 60: Photo of Michele and Thomas Larsen; p. 71: Page from Sotheby's catalog containing locket at auction; p. 74: Photo of Ira Brilliant and Dr. Guevara (speaking), medium close-up; p. 78: Beethoven composing at his piano, based on a painting by Hermann Junker; p. 84: Beethoven at the piano by Moritz Rödig; p. 95: Photograph of the largest skull fragment that consists of two pieces glued together, from the collection of Paul and Joan Kaufmann; p. 96: Graph, X-ray florescence intensity from Ph in hair; p. 97: Three graphs, Radiomicrographs of the region of three of Beethoven's hairs; p. 103: Beethoven on his deathbed, engraving by J. Adé based on a painting by Wilhelm Lindenschmit; p. 105: Beethoven's gravesite in the Währinger Cemetery in Vienna; p. 106: Beethoven in his study by Carl Bernard Schloesser.

Index

Pages numbers in *italics* refer to illustrations.